THE
AMERICA 2051
PROJECT

A NON-POLITICAL PLAN
TO FIX OUR POLITICAL SYSTEM

BY
JAMES M. PAULINO

Flour
City
Press

ROCHESTER, NEW YORK

The America 2051 Project, Inc. is a non-profit organization created to help We the People on the road to an Article V Constitutional Convention (America's second, in fact).

All proceeds from this book will support the Project and its work, like paying college students to contact 7,421 local representatives across 50 states and ask their position on an Article V convention, or maintaining a website (America2051.com) with information about those local candidates at election time, along with fill-in-the-blank legislative documents and other helpful tools for voters.

This book is for educational purposes, and the images contained herein are for the "fair use" purposes of criticism, comment, teaching, scholarship and research, as allowed under 17 U.S.C. § 107. I do not claim any right to use these, and the images are contained without permission, except for the back cover photo by Vasiliy Baziuk. If you object to these uses, and would like to take money away from the non-profit, please email scrooge@America2051.com. Everyone else can feel free to copy this book however you'd like, except for making money.

(CC BY-NC 4.0) 2015 The America 2051 Project, Inc.
ISBN: 978-0-9970696-9-3
Library of Congress Control Number: 2015921110
Flour City Press, Rochester, New York

To the millions of Americans who are involved in their communities, vote, and want to leave this nation in better shape than they found it.

Special thanks to these Americans
who helped get this Project started:

Adam, Bob, Brad, Brian, Chris, Christin, Danielle, Dad,
Dan, Elaine, Eric, Grace, Greg, Jim, Joey, John, Katie,
Laura, Linda, Mary, Mom, Mom, Natalie, Nick, Nicole,
Rachel, Raul, Rick, Sunny, Tim, Tom, Val, Vinnie, Zach,
Team GS & Mr. Naylon

WE THE PEOPLE of the United States, in order to form a MORE PERFECT UNION, establish JUSTICE, insure domestic TRANQUILITY, provide for the Common Defense, promote the General Welfare, and secure the Blessings of LIBERTY to Ourselves and our POSTERITY, do ordain and establish this Constitution for the UNITED STATES OF AMERICA.

Preamble, U.S. Constitution[1]

The basis of our political system is the
right of the people to make and to alter
their constitutions of government.

George Washington
Farewell Address
September 17, 1796[2]

Timeline for Change

2015 - 2020:   Spread the Word
                Organize & Propose Resolutions in 50 States

2020 - 2040:   States Debate and Call for Convention

2040 - 2045:   Constitutional Convention

2045 - 2050:   Ratification

2051:   America's New and Improved Government

2075:   Third Constitutional Convention

2100:   Fourth Constitutional Convention
                (Conventions Every 25 Years)

Contents

PREFACE

Here's the solution we've been waiting for—a peaceful and legal way to update the structure of our federal government, carefully planned by the Founding Fathers, but never once used in the 225 years of our constitutional republic. Yes, that's right, We the People have the power in our hands to stop the perpetual overspending, spiraling debt, constant campaigning, inattentive management, limitless re-election, corporate influence, and perpetual two-party war plaguing Washington DC, and this book lays out the steps to get it done by 2051. First...some preliminary thoughts.

America is We the People.
America is not Washington DC.
Democracy is a process.
We're all in this together.

No one ever said self-government would be easy. On the contrary, over the past two and a half centuries, Americans have disagreed over countless social and political issues, from judicial appointments to education policy to personal income taxation to health insurance, and usually across party lines. But no matter how much we fight, there are some things no American can deny: that we're all created equal, that we all enjoy the same right to live according to our convictions, and that we all deserve a government that is efficient, hard-working, and represents our best interests.

In 1775, there was no American democracy; there were only women and men who dreamed of a nation where they and their children could govern their own affairs without interference from any foreign power. After living under a government that served the interests of only a few, including a hereditary monarch, those early colonists wanted a system that represented the people, and the right to select their own leaders; legislative, executive and judicial. In 1776, those same men and women broke free from the British empire and created the society of their dreams—one where sovereignty rests not on the head of a stranger, but in the hands of the people. And in 1787, it was upon these principles, and the shoulders of those women and men willing to sacrifice their lives for democracy, that our constitutional government was built, not as the leader of society, but as the servant of We the People.

Democracy is not a political issue; it's the continuing journey by We the People toward a More Perfect Union. As for the structure of our government, it's a matter of *political science*, not politics; there are no "Red" or "Blue" checks and balances, there are only We the People, and technical rules for how well our system works. When faced with the political strife of the present, it's easy to forget the goal of this journey, which began centuries before we were born, and will continue (hopefully) for centuries to come. Our struggle as Americans is not against the Republican or Democratic parties—it's the struggle of all free people toward a just society, where the rights of every citizen are protected, and government is streamlined, balanced, and dedicated to the interests of the governed.

I believe in America, and in the fundamental principles on which she was founded. For a while, though, I fell into the trap of thinking that Liberty and Justice for all were the gifts we received from our democratically elected leaders, as opposed to the virtues We the People strive for in our daily lives. It was the American fairy tale: if I were a good citizen all year long, Jolly Old Uncle Sam would come down the chimney the night before the Fourth of July bringing freedom and fireworks for me and my friends. Of course I saw problems in Washington DC, but I had faith that the political system would work itself out…like the free market…and that we just needed new leadership to point us in the right direction. So I got involved, interning in the House of Representatives, working as the statewide coordinator for a US Senate race, and campaigning (and voting) for my politicians of choice.

Election after election and candidate after candidate, I slowly watched our government slide toward complete dysfunction. Despite spirited campaign speeches and very convincing promises, our representatives used more and more power to help themselves and their donors at our expense—including the ones I supported. No matter how hard I worked, things only got worse, and like millions of other Americans, I felt helpless, and gave up trying to make a difference when it came to our government.

Deep down, though, I knew that America did work at some point in the past, and I was convinced that the principles of freedom, equality and self-government are as true today as in 1776. As I became less and less involved in the political process, I spent more and more time reading about the Framers of the Constitution, and appreciating the genius of their revolution and the balanced system of limited government they created. It was then that I finally realized Liberty and Justice start at home, with We the People, and not in Washington DC. (It was also when I understood the full potential of the Article V ("Five") Convention.)

The American experiment in self-government did not end in 1776; it continues today, and as voting citizens, we each have a role to play. So…why a Project? Because the only way to achieve change is for We the People *to do something* —to look past the current two-party strife, stop waiting for a political savior, and start working together with our fellow Americans toward our common good. Progress does not come from repeating the same actions, debating the same issues and complaining about the same candidates year after year and election after election. Just like in 1776, progress comes from doing something different than was done in the

Frederick Douglass   Susan B. Anthony

past. Well, here is a plan for something completely different: legal, peaceful, step-by-step, and (hopefully) in an easy-to-read format.

I was born and raised in Rochester, New York, the stomping grounds of real American heroes like Frederick Douglass and Susan B. Anthony, whose *ideas* and *actions* were catalysts for revolutionary change. Growing up, we were proud of Rochester's history of innovation—Kodak film, Xerox copiers, Western Union, USA Today, Bausch & Lomb, Ray-Ban Sunglasses and, of course, Wegmans—and we aspired to the common motto of New York State and the University of Rochester: *Always Improving*.[3] That's the mission of America, not to rest on our oars and ride the current created by our forebears, but to continue their work in bringing liberty and justice to ourselves and to the world. Since writing this, I've been given a number of articles and books on the Article V process, including a book by fellow lawyer Mark Levin with his own proposed amendments.[4] We all want to see Washington DC get better; this is my humble attempt to help make it happen.

To my older readers, this Project is about your children, your grandchildren, and the future of the land I know you love as much as I do. You have the experience and wisdom needed to design a system that avoids the abuses of power seen during your lifetime. You may not enjoy the fruits of our labor, and you may question whether change like this is even possible, but you know that freedom is worth fighting for, and that we're duty-bound to use our right to vote to protect America, and to ensure her health for years to come.

To my younger readers, an improved system of federal government is possible within your lifetime, and you have the imagination, energy and networking skills needed to see this Project through to completion. Since our founding, each generation has made its unique contributions to America, from the earliest colonists to the Western Expansion to the supporters of prohibition to the free love movement of the 1960s. We have yet, however, to produce a generation since George Washington that thinks critically about the structure of government, and embarks on a comprehensive grassroots nation-wide plan to, in the words of our Constitution, "form a More Perfect Union." If we pull this off, if we can put our nation's future ahead of our present, short term interests, if we can fulfill the Founder's vision to maintain a government that is responsive to We the People, and if we can produce the world's first comprehensive and totally bloodless political revolution, history will refer to us as America's Greatest Generation.

None of us deserves America; we are *all* the beneficiaries of the sacrifice and dedication of those who came before us. We owe it to them, to ourselves, to our posterity, and to the rest of the world to ensure that humanity's greatest experiment in democratic self-government does not fail, but continues for another 225 years.

Let's form a more perfect union.

—Thanksgiving 2015

The Constitution was made for the people
and not the people for the Constitution!

Theodore Roosevelt
Coal Mine Strike, 1902[5]

AMERICA, WE HAVE A PROBLEM...
AND A SOLUTION

AFTER YEARS of listening to my family complain about politicians in Washington DC at countless holidays, birthdays, graduations, pool parties, school concerts, and Sunday dinners, it finally dawned on me—the problem is with the system itself, and our elected representatives are only playing by the rules of the game. I was driving home after one of those awkward-ending conversations (where everyone identifies the same problem, argues over how to solve it, and eventually shrugs their shoulders believing change is beyond their reach) and, after decades agonizing over which candidate will set America on the right path, I realized that no politician can save us: we need to *update the structure* of our federal government to add additional checks, balances, and consequences for our public servants.

The reason our leaders spend and borrow without limit is that no limits exist. The same goes for accepting millions from corporations in political contributions, constant campaigning for re-election, and frustrating progress by voting the party line. For two centuries, we have fought tooth-and-nail for our candidates of choice, and our federal government has only worsened. So, while I was driving home that afternoon, after years of complaints, it struck me like lightning—Don't hate the players; change the rules of the game.

After 225 years, politicians have become experts in using our constitutional system for their own ends. Just as the best athletes go pro, the best politicians go to Washington DC. And, just like sports, there have been advances to help politicians become even more effective at the game, like high-speed travel, full-time campaign staff, constant polling, image consultants, mass mailings, 24-hour news, and now, social media. As a result, our nation is run by folks so skilled in two-party war that government shuts down from time to time,[6] so eager to win re-election that they spend countless hours campaigning instead of doing real work, and so short-sighted that we are $18 trillion in debt, and growing.[7]

The Framers of our Constitution could not have foreseen the realities of modern political life, but they did understand human nature, and they knew that in a legitimate democracy, power must remain in the hands of the people.[8] After suffering under George III and a Parliament without representation, the earliest Americans were committed to placing We the People first and foremost as the strongest and surest protection against government abuse. Setting out to form a balanced, limited, and workable system that embodied these American ideals was no small task. The first attempt, the Articles of Confederation drafted in 1777 and adopted 1781, didn't really work, so the States had to re-convene and draft a new blueprint in 1787: our Constitution.

We all heard the story in grade school...they spent 127 days during a hot and humid Philadelphia summer working in a stale, closed up Assembly Room, but I doubt many have truly considered the challenging and revolutionary nature of that work—to create an entirely new form of government over a vast area and relatively diverse people. There were few historical examples, so Americans looked to legal theories on the legitimacy of state power, coupled with plain old common sense, as they hammered out the framework for our federal system, one that has survived for more than two centuries, and one that we enjoy today.

Thanks to the action of one very interesting American, I believe our system can adapt to the current excesses in Washington DC, and can do so without any involvement from the Congress, President or Supreme Court. After four months of debate, on Saturday, September 15, 1787, the second-to-last day of the *first* Constitutional Convention, a delegate from Pennsylvania, Gouverneur Morris (that's his first name), made a motion to add a new provision allowing the states to reconvene and propose their own amendments to the Constitution.[9]

Gouverneur Morris
1752-1816

Mr. Morris—the primary author of our Constitution and source of the phrase "We the People"—was a real American hero; although, one the history books have largely ignored.[10] Known for his dark sense of humor, serial romances, and "unstatesmanlike frankness and sarcasm," 23-year-old Gouverneur broke away from his aristocratic and Loyalist family (who volunteered their 1,000-acre Bronx estate for British military use)[11] to join New York's provincial congress in 1775, and drafted the State's first constitution the following year.[12] Despite a significant disability to his right arm caused by boiling water during childhood (his arm was described as "fleshless"[13]) and legal exemption as a legislator, Morris served in the state militia until chosen as a delegate to the Continental Congress in 1778, where he acted as the Continental Army's spokesperson and helped General Washington obtain supplies for the "naked, starved, sick, discouraged" troops in Valley Forge.[14] After the Revolution, Morris promoted reconciliation with former Loyalists, including his own mother, and suffered a second physical limitation—the loss of his leg either in a carriage accident or while trying to escape an irate husband (Morris was known as "the rake that wrote the Constitution").[15] After several years as a lawyer and merchant in Philadelphia, Morris was sent by Pennsylvania as a delegate to the Constitutional Convention of 1787, where he was recognized as having the most brilliant intellect of all the American Founders (Madison acknowledged "the brilliancy of his genius,"[16] while Roosevelt described him as "he who was perhaps the most brilliant, although by no means the greatest, of the whole number" of "the founders of the Constitution"[17]). Gouverneur capped his life of public service as the American minister to France, a US Senator, and *the* founding chairman of the Erie Canal Commission.[18] What an American!

On that second-to-last day of the Convention, 35-year-old Gouverneur stood up on his peg leg and asked his fellow delegates to add language to Article V giving states the power to update the blueprint for the new federal system as they saw fit. Another interesting American, Elbridge Gerry, future Governor of Massachusetts, Fifth Vice President of the United States, and father of Gerrymandering, seconded Morris' motion.[19] James Madison, also credited as an author of the Constitution, balked that it was obvious the states could make their own changes, so the motion passed and the Delegates moved to the next issue for debate.[20] As a result, America now sits as the only superpower (maybe even nation) that allows changes to the federal government from *outside* the system, through the states, and without any involvement (or interference) from Washington DC.

The Article V Convention is the only check and balance We the People have against our common government in Washington DC, and, to be blunt, it's high time we used it. Under Article V, if two-thirds of the state legislatures pass resolutions calling for America's *second* Constitutional Convention, then We the People can send a fresh group of delegates to update the blueprint created in 1787 and propose a new and improved formula for what power the Congress, President and Supreme Court can exercise over us. In the 225 years since ratification, our Constitution has been amended only through the Congress (including the Bill of Rights), and, unsurprisingly, there has been no effort to create additional checks and balances, or to limit the amount of power held by our federal representatives. If American citizens will elect state representatives willing to support an Article V Convention, we can *legally, peacefully,* and *finally* restore the balance of power away from Washington DC, and back in favor of We the People.

This Project is our chance to use the one power the federal government can never take away—our vote in state elections—to bring about real and lasting change in Washington DC. As a voting citizen, you're already part of this Project, whether you realize it or not. The question is, will you vote for it, against it, or not at all...?

The America 2051 Handbook

This book is, at its core, an instruction manual for the Article V process (along with some ideas for what parts of the system could be changed). It paints in broad strokes, and some would say oversimplifies the issues, but this is not a treatise on political philosophy, government theory, or the meaning of life—it's a call to action, and one I think millions of Americans are ready to hear.

Part One: Seven Areas for Change explains *Why* we need an Article V Convention in the first place, and identifies the structural flaws that give our public servants the excess power they have been using to help themselves at our expense. I also include possible solutions in the form of amendments, but my suggestions are just that. The key is to understand that there are flaws in the system, and that We the People have the power to call a Constitutional Convention and make whatever reasonable, calculated and carefully worded changes we want.

Part Two: Step-by-Step Instructions outlines how to successfully call and complete an Article V Convention in four easy steps:

1. Start Spreading the News: Tell everyone you know (and people you don't know) about the Article V process, and that we have the legal power to re-write the rulebook for Washington DC;

2. Lobby your Local Representatives: Persuade a majority of the 7,421 state representatives across the United States to support the Article V process, as well as the leadership in the state legislatures, or else we vote 'em out of office (using candidate information at America2051.com);

3. The State Legislative Process: State representatives must propose, analyze, debate and pass resolutions calling for a limited Article V Convention to solve

specific problems with the current Constitution and identifying the state's proposed delegates; and

4. <u>Convention Time!</u>: Delegates from all 50 states will hold a Convention to propose updates to the structure of our federal government, using the same rules and procedures as George Washington in the Convention of 1787.

The necessary state legislative documents are found in Part Three: Fill-in-the-Blank Documents, as well as tools to spread the word and win support from local representatives, including draft emails, letters, newspaper editorials, elevator speeches, event flyers, and even the America 2051 Party Kit so that you can invite your friends to learn about and celebrate America's *second* Revolution! After Thomas Paine wrote Common Sense, it was up to the People to debate the issues in houses, churches, town halls and taverns across the land, and to collectively charter the new nation's course. This book is a second invitation for Americans to do just that.

A Carefully Limited Convention

This Project is not a free-for-all where every part of our Constitution is up for grabs; it seeks a *limited* convention to propose amendments that solve specific problems, like perpetual overspending, constant campaigning or corporate influence in elections, and nothing more. Everything not expressly identified will be off limits, which is (sort of) how they ran things in 1787: each delegate to the Convention carried special papers from the state legislature defining the power they had to make changes, and what areas were off limits.[21] It will then be up to the delegates to hammer out solutions in the form of proposed amendments, and send the proposals back to the states for ratification.

For the constitutional lawyers and political scientists reading this, there are three safeguards to ensure the Convention will be limited. First, the legislatures will adopt resolutions granting limited public trust in delegates, with authority to propose amendments solving only a specific list of problems. Second, I suggest that each delegate take a sworn oath accepting the public's limited trust, and agreeing to remain within the bounds set by the legislature (or else be subject to criminal prosecution). Third, there's always next time: if we make it to a second Convention and delegates come up with a great idea but aren't authorized to act by the state resolutions, odds are it won't be some doomsday scenario, and we can wait a few more years for the states to call a *third* Constitutional Convention. Even after 225 years, patience remains a virtue.

The following are brief summaries of the seven major problems we could (should) address at a Convention, along with some possible solutions. (Each is discussed in detail in the next section.) At the end of the day, it will be up to the delegates, as our democratic representatives, to propose the amendments, so please consider my suggested solutions merely food for thought. For once, instead of fighting over our differences of opinion, I recommend we celebrate our agreement to change the system, and move full steam ahead in the same direction. Leave the strife for another day—*let's just do something!*

1. Boundaries and Consequences: I was a full-time intern in Congress during college, and if I could compare it to anything, it would be a country club where you do little to no work, and enjoy parties, TV appearances, free meals, celebrity visits, private movie screenings, back-room deals, political intrigue, constant jokes, and plenty of gossip. Elected representatives borrow and spend whatever they want, stay in office as long as possible, vote the party line over 92% of the time,[22] and are at work 50% less than the rest of us.[23] For example, on November 30, 2014, America's national debt reached $18 trillion (over $100,000 per adult) after a one-day increase of $32 billion,[24] and then, two months later, President Obama announced $500 tax rebates for married couples who work.[25] The only way to stop the madness is to limit the power of politicians; I suggest amendments adding spending limits, term limits and attendance requirements, and making representatives ineligible for re-election as a punishment for violations. Yep, if they mess up, then they lose their jobs; it's called accountability.

2. Equal Process for Equal Votes: Americans have no Constitutional right to vote in federal elections. And, each state has different eligibility rules and ballots, so the act of voting in federal elections isn't the same across the 50 States. Remember Bush v Gore and Butterfly Ballots in Palm Beach County, Florida? Lack of uniformity caused a political circus and legal nightmare. If we all share an equal right to vote in national elections, then why is the act of voting different across America? (States, of course, should keep their own internal rules for state elections.) I suggest amendments creating a uniform system for voting in federal elections, with automatic eligibility when you turn 18 (just like the draft), and overseen by a non-partisan organization through the Supreme Court, similar to Canada's independent elections commission, which helps keep party politics out of the electoral process.

3. An All-American Democratic Process: It costs $2 billion to elect a President, $20 million a Senator, and $2.5 million a Member of the House.[26] That money is not coming from the 300 million Americans who make up this country: only 0.23% of us ever contribute more than $200 per election cycle (yes, less than one percent).[27] As of August 2015, for example, fewer than 400 of America's wealthiest families made nearly 50% of all donations to the 2016 presidential candidates.[28]

The sad fact is that businesses and the super-rich are bankrolling our democracy and buying our public servants, like CitiGroup (which contributed $2,702,288 to candidates in 2012, including $491,249 to Mitt Romney *and* $209,452 to Barack Obama, and spent $5,520,000 in lobbying[29]), Honeywell (which contributed $3,000,000 to political campaigns in 2010[30]), and Wells Fargo (which spent $14,449,001 on federal lobbying and donations from 2013-2014[31]), or individuals like Michael Bloomberg and Thomas and Kathryn Steyer, who reportedly donated $28 and $75 million respectively during the 2014 election cycle.[32] As my Congresswoman Louise Slaughter recently said at a round-table discussion, every politician has a sugar daddy.

Unless the Supreme Court overturns its prior decisions regarding campaign finance (which is highly unlikely) the only way to reduce the influence of money in politics is through an amendment that completely re-writes the rules on how campaigns are funded. If only American citizens can vote in American elections, then I suggest that only American citizens should be allowed to influence elections with financial contributions. Likewise, if every American has an equal right to vote, then we should all have an equal opportunity to make our voices heard by capping the total amount of political donations, as opposed to allowing the super-wealthy to have a louder voice than the middle class through unlimited contributions. And, as every minute campaigning for re-election is a minute away from real work, I suggest we establish ground-rules for federal campaigns and place limits on how much a politician can spend on wasteful commercials and flyers that are all show and no substance.

4. Using Taxes to Curb Government Spending: Matt Barrett, the nicest law professor in America, taught me that the tax code has nothing to do with the laws of nature: it's an entirely made up system, and can be used however the political forces deem beneficial. The current system, with its arbitrary rates of 10%, 15%, 25%, 28%, 33%, 35% and 39.6%, isn't linked to the amount government spends, so taxpayers don't feel the impact of runaway debt.[33] In 2014, government expenditures were almost $500 million *more* than revenue, but We the People didn't notice because the tax rates stayed the same.[34] These rates also skyrocket 300% from $1 to $413,200 of earned income, but flatline with 0% increase after that, placing the heaviest burden on folks earning under $400,000 a year.[35] Oh, and it costs $13 billion each year to run the IRS, which our elected representatives conveniently use to target political opponents.[36] The solution, I believe, is to link the tax rate to how much the government spends (variable), to eliminate the regulatory labyrinth using a standard rate without deductions or credits (flat), and to distribute the rate increase evenly across all dollars, and not just on the middle class (progressive), i.e. "a variable progressive flat tax."

5. Divide and Conquer: The President has more responsibility than any one person can handle. In addition to maintaining global security, running the military, handling international affairs, appointing judges and diplomats, and combating world health and environmental problems, the President is expected to manage infrastructure, education, energy, retirement, taxes, urban housing, elderly care, medical insurance, minimum wages, space exploration, scientific research, drug trafficking, immigration, and racism here at home. So, let's divide the President's duties into two separate offices—the popularly elected President can handle the military, foreign affairs, judicial and diplomatic appointments, and serve as Head of State, while a "National Secretary" appointed by the President and confirmed by Congress can handle domestic affairs, like bridges and the Post Office. It's what 27 other democracies already do, including France and Germany.[37] In other words, let's replace the Vice President with a domestic leader responsive to We the People through our Congress.

And...We the People elect the President—we do not elect any "First Spouse." Yet, we spend millions in taxpayer dollars each year for the First Spouse's 20+ person staff and their first-class travel around the globe. I say, it's time to put some limits on supporting the "First Spouse" before things really get out of control.

6. Breaking the Two-Party Deadlock: Today, 42% of Americans identify as independents, while only 25% as Republicans and 31% as Democrats.[38] I'm part of that 42%, and am tired of watching the far left and far right nominate virtually all candidates for office, leaving those of us who fall in the middle little real chance to be represented. America is the *only* modern democracy with two political parties in the national legislature, and in our winner-take-all system, where we cast a single vote for one representative in Congress, we will *always* have only two parties. (Political scientists call this Duverger's Law.) This two-party system has crippled progress, with representatives voting the party line over 92%[39] of the time, leading to government shut downs for 16 days in 2013,[40] and 21 days from 1995 to 1996.[41]

In 1819, 40 years after our Constitution was adopted, a new system of voting was invented that allows more than two political parties to emerge. Under "proportional representation" rules, if we change our ballot to give us two votes per Congressional district—one for a representative and the second for a party—we can progress to a "multi-party" system, finally giving moderates a voice in Congress, and (hopefully) settling the centuries-old two-party war.

7. Regularly Scheduled Justice: Every presidential election, we *guess* which supreme court judges *could* retire or die, and how each candidate *might* make appointments. This uncertainty distracts from the range of important issues to address during the presidential campaign process. Mandatory retirement for federal judges at 75 (or after 20 years on the bench, whichever comes first) will eliminate the speculation over possible appointments during campaigns, and, hopefully, allow fresh legal minds to keep our courts agile and responsive to a changing world.

The Senate, responsible for approving presidential nominations to federal courts, has infused even more politics into the process, with confirmation now taking 223 days during the Obama administration, as opposed to 60 under President Reagan.[42] We need functioning courts for a functioning democracy, and we must limit the time Senators can manipulate confirmation for their own political advantage. I suggest that, if the Senate does not vote on a nomination within 60 days, the judge is deemed confirmed, and if the President does not fill a vacancy within 30 days, the Speaker of the House can make the nomination.

How does Article V work?

When Thomas Jefferson read the new Constitution, he didn't like it. "There are indeed some faults which revolted me a good deal in the first moment," he told James Madison from Paris in 1788. "But," Jefferson continued," we must be contented to travel on towards perfection, step by step."[43] How do we travel toward perfection? We update the system on a regular and continual basis...through the Article V Convention.

I have no idea why they don't teach this in civics class, but the Article V process consists of five easy steps, and is handled entirely through the states, without any help (or interference) from Congress, the President or Supreme Court:

1. Local representatives must propose resolutions calling for an Article V convention in state legislative chambers across the United States (a fill-in-the-blank resolution is

Article V, United States Constitution

The Congress, whenever two thirds of both houses shall deem it necessary, shall propose amendments to this Constitution, <u>or</u>, *on the application of the legislatures of two thirds of the several states, shall call a convention for proposing amendments, which, in either case, shall be valid to all intents and purposes, as part of this Constitution, when ratified by the legislatures of three-fourths of the several states,* or by conventions in three fourths thereof, as the one or the other mode of ratification may be proposed by the Congress; provided that no amendment which may be made prior to the year one thousand eight hundred and eight shall in any manner affect the first and fourth clauses in the ninth section of the first article; and that no state, without its consent, shall be deprived of its equal suffrage in the Senate.

Article Five in Plain English

Option One: Through Congress	Option Two: Through Convention
290 Representatives (two-thirds of the House) and 67 Senators (two-thirds of the Senate) pass a joint resolution proposing amendments, which are sent to the states for their consideration.	34 state legislatures (two-thirds) pass resolutions calling for a convention of state delegates to propose amendments. The states hold the convention somewhere far away from Washington, DC, where delegates hammer out proposed amendments, which are then sent to the states for their consideration.

provided on page 150).

2. A majority of representatives in 34 state legislatures must vote in support of the resolutions (after research and analysis by committees, and after the leadership allows debate and a full vote).

3. Each state's legislative clerk must send a stamped copy of the resolution to the National Archivist in Washington, DC, who is a form of national clerk to receive and record documents for the American people. (Yes, the United States actually have someone whose job is to handle amendments to the Constitution.)[44]

4. When 34 resolutions are published by the Archivist in the Statutes at Large and Federal Register, all 50 states are legally authorized to send delegates to meet as they did in 1787 and propose upgrades and revisions to the system.

5. The delegates send their proposed amendments to the National Archivist to coordinate the ratification process.

The States will have the last word through ratification, which will serve as yet another check to ensure the delegates do not overstep their authority at the Convention.

The key to start this process already exists—your vote in state elections. If we elect local representatives willing to call for a Convention, We the People simply cannot fail! Thanks to the magic of the Internet, voters can find out if an incumbent (or challenger) will support a Convention by simply typing in their home address at America2051.com (after the Project contacts all 7,421 representatives...which could take some time). And, with email and social media, We the People have greater influence over local elections than ever before. Without a doubt, it is easier to impact a *local* election than a *federal* one, because our local districts have fewer voters, and our local representatives live among us as part-time legislators and part-time citizens, as opposed to the full-time politicians in Washington DC.

It may seem frightening to re-write the rulebook for Washington DC, but, apart from the bits protecting our rights (which are inalienable and therefore completely off limits), there really is nothing special about a constitution. In fact, any organization can have one, from garden clubs in North Dakota to bowling clubs in Tennessee.[45] Constitutions are like blueprints, or recipes, with a list of ingredients and set of instructions for creating a house, cake, organization, or fully functioning government. And, like any recipe, a constitution can be changed, and hopefully improved, over the years.

Today, there are 79 different democracies in the world, each with its own recipe for how government operates.[46] There is no reason We the People in America cannot improve our system and adapt it to the political landscape and realities of modern living. As Jefferson warned, Americans must "not to go backwards instead of forwards to look for improvement, to believe that government, religion, morality, and every other science were in the highest perfection in ages of the darkest ignorance, and that nothing can ever be devised more perfect than what was established by our forefathers..."[47] If nature teaches us anything, unless we adapt, we jeopardize our own survival.

Seriously, 2051?

If Americans make this the key issue in State elections, it will take no longer than ten years to call the United States' second Constitutional Convention. But, this Project is about much more than changing the Constitution once and then slowly sliding back into complacency; it's about our *continuing* journey toward a More Perfect Union. This is an opportunity for We the People to imagine what America will look like in the second half of this century if things continue as they have for the past 225 years. More importantly, it's an invitation to ask ourselves—What are we wiling to do *today* to ensure America's strength for centuries into the *future*? Some of us may never see 2051, but like the Framers of the

Constitution, we have a moral obligation to think strategically about how we can ensure America's survival for generations to come. 2051 is a gentle reminder that America is greater than any of the citizens alive today, and that we must plan ahead if this democracy will retain its strength at home and influence around the world.

But...2051 also is a deadline for action, before our nation's spiraling debt and two-party war reach the point of no return. When our federal government cannot even keep the Statue of Liberty open, we should realize that things are getting pretty bad.[48] If We the People do not place real limits on Washington DC by the middle of this century, odds are it will be too late. The recent tumult in Greece is an unfortunate reminder that nothing lasts forever. The Greek empire was the cradle of Western civilization and used to rule the world; now they're going bankrupt.[49] America cannot survive under its current management rules; they must be adapted to the 21st Century, and remain flexible well into the future.

When it comes to calling the second Constitutional Convention, the only variable is you—the voter—and your dedication to fixing America. From here, it's all in your hands. Once Americans understand the simplicity of this solution, and the amount of power we have over Washington DC, this Project will succeed. It might just take some time to pull it off.

Of course, there will be obstacles—there are always haters—but there is nothing We the People cannot handle if we work together. First, Washington DC probably won't be happy, and the lobbying groups embedded in the Capitol will attempt to spread their money and influence across America in an effort to choke progress. The solution is to move full steam ahead and put unwavering pressure on our state representatives until they pass resolutions calling for a Constitutional Convention. The genius of Article V is that it requires people from every part of the nation to act, making it harder for any interest or lobby to hijack the entire process. Lobbyists may have a choke-hold on the federal government, but their tentacles do not (yet) extend to cities across the United States like Wichita, Memphis, Juneau, Las Vegas, Chattanooga, Kalamazoo and New Orleans. And, as explained above, this Project avoids any involvement from the Congress, President or Supreme Court. For once, Washington DC must follow *our lead*.

The second and perhaps larger obstacle is that state legislatures might block progress, afraid of how changes to Washington DC could affect them. If We the People call for term limits on Congress, what's to say we won't demand change in our state capitols? Well, two responses. First, state representatives need to get over themselves—they are servants of the public, chosen by We the People to do what's best for us. Second, We the People must target these representatives at election time, and unrelentingly demand change, or else vote them out of office. We have the power to overcome this obstacle—we simply must vote to do it.

I'm sure there are more hurdles…but I'm an optimist. Go big or go home. If we aim for it, and if we realize our duty to America and our responsibility to vote, it'll happen sooner or later. This Project should be a walk in the park compared to the Revolution of 1776.

Less Conversation, More Action

We have debated the issues long enough. Now is the time for We the People to look past the current dividing lines (arbitrarily) drawn across our society, work with our fellow Americans toward our common good, and take one giant leap, together, toward change.

We will need judges, political scientists, veterans, historians, philosophers, business owners, teachers, students…and everyone else across the nation to debate and understand the problems, and to develop realistic solutions. Thankfully, this isn't America's first rodeo. We have 225 years of experience under the current system on which to base changes to election rules, taxation, terms of office, Presidential power, political donations, and the two-party system. Plus, James Madison left us a 650-page record of the first Constitutional Convention, complete with rules of procedure and notes from the debates. Once we get to the Convention, assuming we send qualified delegates, we can follow in the footsteps of the intellectual giants who went before us. If the rules were good enough for George Washington (President of the first Convention), they're good enough for me.

But…We the People _must work together_ if any of this is to be accomplished. I cannot overstate the simple truth that, regardless of all of the dividing lines drawn across these United States on TV, in the press, and in popular culture, we really are all 100% Americans, and we're all in this together. I grew up in a "mixed" family with divorces and re-marriages

and step- and half- and adopted brothers and sisters (six of us in total), and I've learned that the only lasting foundation for true brotherhood and sisterhood is mutual respect and commitment, through the ups and downs of life, hard times and good times, and any number of fights, hurt feelings, and disagreements. The only way for the United States to survive to 2051 and beyond is for We the People to make a conscious decision to work together, not because it feels good, but because we are all part of the same family, and, for better or worse, we're stuck with each other. In my opinion, that's one of the most beautiful things about these United States of America.

All we need to start the Article V bloodless revolution is your vote in state elections. It's not a difficult task, and it's something you should be doing anyway. If proud citizens across America will coordinate locally in their state elections and choose representatives who will call for a constitutional convention, then we finally can make the changes we have all dreamed of...a government that doesn't overspend, listens to its people, balances the budget, is free from corporate influence, and engages in dialogue instead of two-party strife. Americans from all walks of life (and all political parties) must participate for this Project to succeed, and We the People can find common ground in the principles of Liberty and Justice for all, the same principles that launched this great American enterprise in self-government in the first place.

So, if you'd like to read about what I think we should change, and my proposed fixes, turn the page. Or, if you're ready for change now, and you want to see how to call a Convention, feel free to flip ahead to page 107.

America, let's choose our own adventure!

PART ONE:

SEVEN AREAS
FOR
CHANGE

(AND SOME PROPOSED SOLUTIONS)

"Trust us, we're Politicians!"

BOUNDARIES & CONSEQUENCES

At the end of the day, our "public servants" are only human, and if we were in their shoes, we might even act the same way they do. Human nature creates a fundamental conflict of interest for all elected representatives: while they should diligently perform what's best for We the People, politicians have an obvious interest in keeping their jobs. To survive in an elected office, indeed to thrive, politicians must:

1. Spend as much time as possible getting re-elected;
2. Follow the party's orders to maintain committee assignments and receive the party's endorsement and financial support at election time;
3. Stay in the job as long as possible, because we all need jobs, and, for this one, the longer you're there, the more power you have to control the nation; and
4. Spend as much taxpayer money on local projects and other legislation to help raise campaign dollars and secure votes.

Unfortunately, what's good for a politician's career isn't necessarily what's good for We the People. Should I do what's best for the country, or should I do what's best for my re-election chances? Should I work hard, or should I go to parties and fundraisers where I'm the guest of honor? Should

President's Proposed Total Spending
(Fiscal Year 2015)

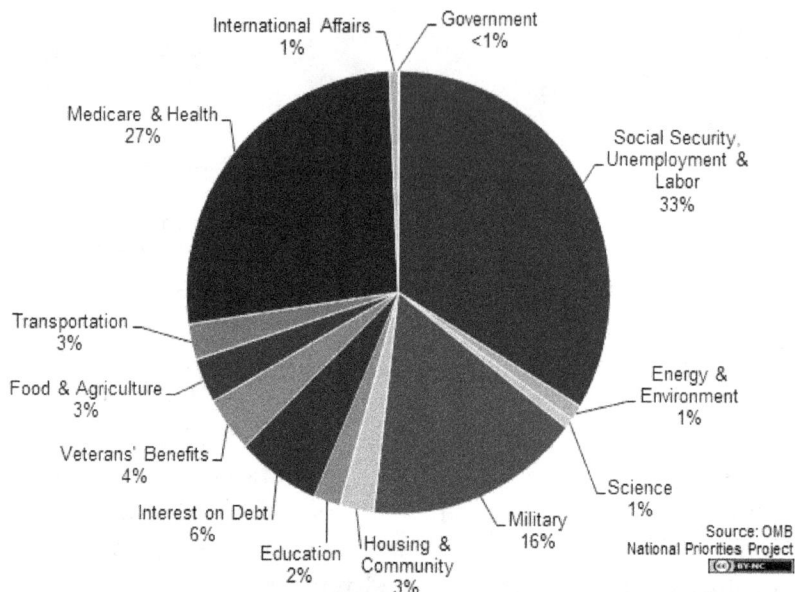

International Affairs 1%
Government <1%
Medicare & Health 27%
Social Security, Unemployment & Labor 33%
Transportation 3%
Energy & Environment 1%
Food & Agriculture 3%
Veterans' Benefits 4%
Interest on Debt 6%
Science 1%
Military 16%
Education 2%
Housing & Community 3%

Source: OMB
National Priorities Project

Projected Mandatory and Discretionary Spending and Interest on Federal Debt
(Fiscal Year 2015)

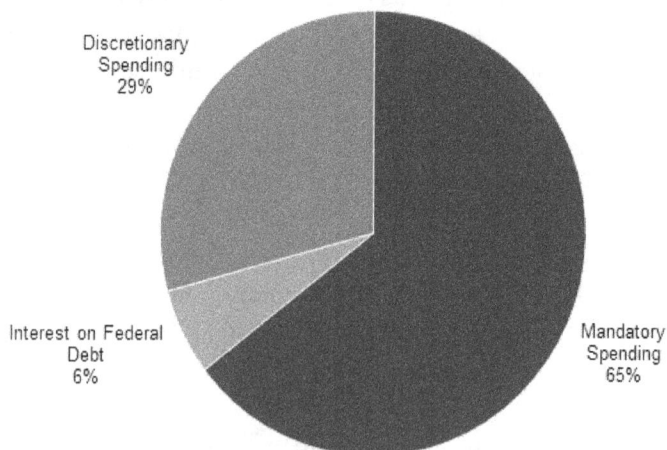

Discretionary Spending 29%
Interest on Federal Debt 6%
Mandatory Spending 65%

Source: OMB
National Priorities Project

I lift restrictions on the chemical company who paid for my campaign, or should I protect the citizens who live downstream from the proposed production facility? In Washington DC, conflicts of interest abound.

It's naïve to trust that our elected representatives are all selfless, honest, and responsible public servants willing to sacrifice their careers and honor for We the People. Politicians are merely human, and, like the rest of us, generally do what is in their own best interests. So, until we can elect angels to run the government, we must add constitutional limits *and* punishments to change the incentive structure in Washington DC, and take away the opportunities for our federal representatives to help themselves at our expense.

Spending Limits and Eligibility for Re-Election

When it comes to spending and borrowing, few of us read the thousands of pages in annual budgets or watch where every penny is appropriated throughout the year. Instead, we trust the "goodness" of our public servants to keep the People's interests first. As a result of this (blind) trust, our government spends a whole lot more money than it makes. In 2014, for example, expenditures were $3.5 trillion, and tax revenues were $3.02 trillion, so Washington DC borrowed the $500 billion needed to cover the gap.[50] In fact, since 1960, the federal budget has been balanced only five times.[51] After decades of overspending, We the People now pay $229 billion in annual interest (and growing) to banks and foreign governments,[52] including to China and Japan who respectively own $1.223 and $1.224 trillion of our debt (government securities).[53]

It's our money these politicians are spending. Actually, they've spent all of our money, borrowed $18 trillion in our names, and continue to wrack up additional debt, which we will have to pay back…with interest. Today, that interest is over 6% of the entire federal budget—more than Education and Veterans Benefits combined—all because there were no limits on what former Congresses and Presidents could borrow and spend.[54] Tax dollars should be used for what America needs. And, if it's borrowed money, it should be *only* for the absolute bare necessities. The reality is quite opposite. We the People have paid military contractors $37 for a screw, $7,622 for a coffee maker, and $640 for a toilet seat,[55] and those military contractors have donated to political campaigns. The government spends billions bailing out financial institutions and car manufacturers who give CEOs million dollar bonuses ($1.6 billion of the bank bailout went to bank executives,[56] and $500 million to auto-industry executives[57]), who in turn contribute to political campaigns. As for local projects like new stadiums and public art, taxpayers really don't need those, but we gladly accept them because, who wouldn't? Unless there are constitutional limits, politicians will continue to spend as much as they can to help their own political futures. And, unless there are limits on borrowing, they will keep raising the imaginary "debt ceiling" and put future generations into as much financial bondage as they want.[58] Under the current rules, there simply is no incentive for politicians to keep their hands out of the cookie jar.

The solution to this one is pretty simple: place limits on spending and borrowing. I suggest an amendment requiring Congress to pass a balanced budget by a fixed date, where expenses are less than revenues, and if they fail, they are ineligible for re-election (or perhaps they don't get paid). Of course, Congress can borrow in times of national crisis, but only when approved by a supermajority in both Houses of Congress. We should also include a plan to pay off the current debt over the next 100 years or so. Unfortunately, after decades of waste, we may need to make some tough choices about what expenses really matter, and what is not sustainable…

Proposed Amendment:

The fiscal budget for each calendar year shall be passed by the House of Representatives no later than the first of October of the preceding year. The fiscal budget must be balanced, as passed, such that expenditures do not exceed revenues from the variable-progressive-flat income tax.

If a balanced fiscal budget is not timely passed, the leadership of all parties having representation of at least 10% of the House shall be ineligible for re-election.

The balanced fiscal budget must include mandatory expenditure on government debt as follows: twice the scheduled payment of interest on all outstanding loans, or seven-and-one-half percent of the balanced fiscal budget, whichever is lesser.

The government may borrow beyond the budget only upon declaration of National Emergency or War by a seventy percent super-majority of the House and Senate. The House and Senate shall require from the President [or National Secretary] a detailed budget showing every penny being spent, and on what, in obligation to the taxpayer, regardless of the type or purpose of expenditure. The President [or National Secretary] shall not request funding from Congress unless an itemization of every penny spent is provided therewith, and made public.

The President [or National Secretary] shall publish an accounting by January 30th of the preceding fiscal year, and shall contain from each Cabinet Secretary an itemization of all receipts[, or be removed from office].

[See pg. 87 for discussion of National Secretary.]

Term Limits

In the private sector, promotion is generally based on merit: whoever is best at the job is given more responsibility. In Congress, however, promotion comes simply from being there longer than everyone else. The problem with letting the longest serving representatives run things is that they:

1. Lose touch with the people they represent,
2. Monopolize ideas and control debate,
3. Lack a sense of urgency,
4. Follow and unilaterally enforce the party's agenda,
5. Influence the votes of newer representatives, and
6. Avoid living under the laws they enact.

The problem is not that all representatives are in office too long. The average term is only 9.7 years.[59] It's that only a small group of the longest-serving representatives exercise complete control over our Legislative Branch.

My Congresswoman, Louise Slaughter, and the implementation of Obamacare are a perfect example. (No offense intended; she's done great things for America, but there are other people just as qualified for that job.) They called it the Slaughter Solution, where she was able to use a procedural rule to pass something with majority vote (50% +1), when the law required a 60% vote.[60] As a lawyer, I respect her ability to use the rules to help her client; my question is who is her client...the American people, or the party she's served for over 30 years?

I propose 15 year term limits for the House (together with longer three-year terms, discussed below), and 18 years for the Senate, which will provide the following benefits (and more):

1. Maintain a fresh crop of representatives, with new ideas and energy;

2. Provide an end date for service, which should help with time management for large-scale projects (I've only got 15 years to make a difference, and I'm going to do it!);
3. Attract better candidates who aren't looking for careers, but want to serve for a short time and return to civilian life; and
4. Increase accountability, as the representatives will live under the laws they made, and with the neighbors they represented.

<u>Proposed Amendment:</u>

No Member of the House of Representatives shall serve for more than 15 years, or Senator more than 18 years.

<u>113th Congress: 2013-2015 Legislature's Term in Office[61]</u>

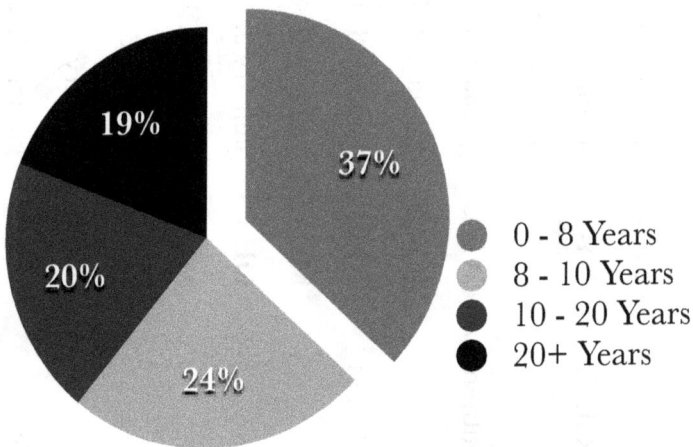

- 0 - 8 Years
- 8 - 10 Years
- 10 - 20 Years
- 20+ Years

113th Congress' Longest Serving Members (July 2015)[1]

John Conyers	MI-13	January 3, 1965	Dean of the House; Ranking Member: Judiciary
Charles B. Rangel	NY-13	January 3, 1971	
Don Young	AK	March 6, 1973	
James Sensenbrenner	WI-05	January 3, 1979	
Hal Rogers	KY-05	January 3, 1981	Chair: Appropriations
Christopher Smith	NJ-04	January 3, 1981	
Steny Hoyer	MD-05	May 19, 1981	Minority Whip
Marcy Kaptur	OH-09	January 3, 1983	
Sander Levin	MI-09	January 3, 1983	Ranking Member: Ways and Means
Joe Barton	TX-06	January 3, 1985	
Pete Visclosky	IN-01	January 3, 1985	
Peter DeFazio	OR-04	January 3, 1987	Ranking Member: Transportation and Infrastructure

[1] http://en.wikipedia.org/wiki/Term_of_office

Mandatory Attendance, with Consequences

When I was in school, they forced me to show up for class by taking attendance. And, for most of my jobs, they made me clock-in, and punished me for being late. It's called accountability, and it's missing in Congress.

The average person works about 2,000 hours each year (40 hours a week x 50 weeks a year, or 250 eight-hour days). To get paid, most people have to show up on time, and remain at work for each of those hours. Congress, on the other hand, is in session around 50% of that amount,[63] an average of 138.5 days, and from what I could see when I was in DC, representatives don't do much work even when they are in session. They don't punch in, and they don't punch out, and they have no deadlines—they just show up when they need to vote…or when the news cameras are ready. The rest of the time, they're generally busy campaigning to keep their jobs. Being in Congress isn't just about voting or being on TV; it's about running America, and it's more than a full-time job.

House of Representatives: Days in Session					
Year	Workdays	Year	Workdays	Year	Workdays
2013	160	2005	122	1997	134
2012	153	2004	110	1996	128
2011	177	2003	138	1995	167
2010	128	2002	126	1994	124
2009	163	2001	146	1993	143
2008	119	2000	139	1992	126
2007	167	1999	139	1991	154
2006	104	1998	119	1990	138

A Typical Day in Congress

District Work Period	Washington, D.C. Work Period
6:15 CT – 9:00 a.m. ET (time zone change): Travel	8:00 – 8:30 a.m.: Meeting with 2011 Congressional Art Competition winner for the 8th District
9:00 – 9:45 a.m. ET: Groundbreaking for Greene County Waste Water Treatment Plant (speaking)	8:30 – 9:30 a.m.: Republican Conference Meeting
	9:30 a.m. – 12:00 p.m.: Transportation & Infrastructure Committee Full Committee Bill Markup
10:00 – 10:50 a.m. ET: CACI Ribbon Cutting and Open House at WestGate (speaking)	10:00 a.m. – 12:00 p.m.: Education & the Workforce Committee Full Committee Bill Markup on H.R. 2218, "Empowering Parents through Quality Charter Schools Act"
11:00 a.m. – 12:30 p.m. ET: Meeting with RADIUS Indiana at Crane Credit Union	10:00 a.m. – 12:00 p.m.: Science, Space, and Technology Full Committee Hearing on "NOAA's Climate Service Proposal"
1:00 – 2:00 p.m. ET: Meeting and Tour of URS at WestGate at Crane Technology Park	11:30 a.m.: Legislative Business begins on the Floor of the U.S. House of Representatives (votes throughout day)
2:15 – 3:15 p.m. ET: Meeting and Tour of SAIC at WestGate at Crane Technology Park	12:30 – 1:30 p.m.: Republican Study Committee weekly staff meeting
	2:00 – 2:30 p.m.: GOP Doctors' Caucus Press Conference
3:15 ET – 4:30 p.m. CT (time change): Travel	3:00 – 4:15 p.m.: Department of Defense Value Engineering Awards at the Pentagon where Naval Surface Warfare Center, Crane division received two awards
5:00 – 6:00 p.m. CT: Constituent meetings in Evansville District Office	4:15 – 5:15 p.m.: Constituent Meetings in Office
	5:30 – 7:00 p.m.: Votes

But, aren't representatives extremely productive while in Washington DC (a mere) three days a week, from Tuesday through Thursday? Based on Rep. Buschon's "Typical Day in Congress," it doesn't seem so.[64] Instead, it seems our public servants cram 13.5 hours of events into an 11-hour day, with up to three meetings at a time, 1.75 hours at awards ceremonies, 0.5 hour on press, 8.5 hours on committee and caucus meetings, 1.0 hour listening to constituents with problems, and then 1.5 hours chatting on the House floor and voting the party line. No time studying laws, reviewing government budgets, analyzing military spending, or doing any other planning for America's future—no substantive work of any kind. And, because every weekend is long, Members have plenty of time to campaign back at home from Friday through Monday.

What about committee meetings? Even if a representative is triple-booked, that's real work, right? I've sat through my fair share, including up on the stage in Ways and Means, and they're mostly a joke. Witnesses evade questions or downright lie, and politicians read statements prepared by others, typically speaking to TV cameras in otherwise empty rooms. Members pop in and out to give their sound bite, and find on their desks, where the cameras can't see, pre-written statements drafted by staff members. While waiting to read their scripts, the representatives did crossword puzzles, checked their email, and doodled. Of course, there are some stand-out public servants, but not enough to fix the problem.

The solution may be unorthodox, but makes common sense: change the job description to require mandatory attendance for 10-hour days at least 200 days a year, or else a representative will be ineligible for re-election (or possibly removed from office). The Supreme Court could appoint an attendance clerk, like a homeroom teacher, to keep records and to impose consequences for truants. If a representative is sick, the clerk will accept a doctor's note, just like every high school in America. If this sounds childish, then why do millions of Americans have timecards at their jobs? And, Congress worked just fine when representatives actually sat in the legislative chamber and dealt with issues instead of constantly campaigning for re-election. Just as in any other profession, if we want to attract employees who are willing to put in long hours, we need to change the job description.

Proposed Amendment:

The House and Senate shall be in session at least 200 days each year, and shall have a morning and afternoon part for each day. Each day, the Chamber shall be in session at least 8 hours, with a one-hour break for lunch. Each Chamber shall have mandatory Roll Call at the beginning and end of each morning and afternoon session. If a Rep. or Sen. is absent from more than 10 daily sessions, except for committee or other business assignments, as approved by House Clerk, the Rep. or Sen. shall be ineligible for re-election [or removed from office]. The Clerk of the Supreme Court shall appoint each calendar year an Attendance Clerk to keep track of Members on a daily basis, and to report the attendance to each State's Board of Elections. If the Speaker of the House fails to call the House to order at least 200 days each year, the Speaker and Majority Leader shall be ineligible for re-election [or removed from office].

Open-Source Government

Our federal government spends nearly $4 trillion each year, but there is little analysis on exactly where that money goes. Unless We the People know how and where the government is using our money, how can we appreciate the amount of waste and special interest expenditures? Like most other things having to do with Washington DC, it seems that we rely on the honor system to ensure our public servants are being good stewards of our tax dollars, but, if human nature has taught us anything, it's that the honor system just doesn't work. Just imagine what you would do with the company credit card if no one would ever find out...

In the computer world, some software is "open source," including the original Apple I system, which means everyone has access to the data, anyone can improve on the system, and everyone enjoys the benefits from the collective effort to make the program better.[65] The key to "open source" is to provide open access to the basic information, and allow regular folks to review, analyze, and make improvements. As Apple's co-inventor Steve Wozniak said, open source lets you take your own genius and make the program better.[66]

We can apply this same principle to federal expenditures. The technology exists for all federal employees to post their receipts on-line within one week, along with an explanation justifying the expense (except for anything posing a security risk). With all due respect to government employees (my dad worked for our county for 30 years), they are "public servants," and should be accountable to the taxpayer just the same as any employee is responsible to a boss.

We the People should be allowed to see where every penny of our money goes, including those Secret Service parties in South America.[67] Regular Americans can serve as a "check" on the government by "crunching the numbers" and identifying areas of gross waste (maybe high schools and colleges could make this a class project). Information is

Years Between Elections (Lower House of Legislature)

Two	USA
Three	Australia, El Salvador, Mexico, Nauru, New Zealand, Philippines
Four	Albania, Andorra, Angola, Argentina, Bahrain, Belarus, Belgium, Bosnia and Herzegovina, Brazil, Bulgaria, Chad, Chile, Columbia, Costa Rica, Croatia, Czech Republic, Congo, Denmark, Dominican Republic, Equador, Estonia, Finland, Georgia, Ghana, Greece, Guatemala, Haiti, Honduras, Hungary, Iceland, Iran, Iraq, Israel, Japan, Jordan, Kiribati, Kuwait, Latvia, Lebanon, Liechtenstein, Lithuania, Macedonia, Marshall Islands, Moldova, Mongolia, Montenegro, Netherlands, Niger, Norway, Oman, Paulau, Palestine, Poland, Portugal, Romania, Serbia, Slovakia, Slovenia, Solomon Islands, South Korea, Spain, Sweden, Switzerland, Syria, Sao Tome, Taiwan, Thailand, Turkey, Tuvalu, Ukraine, Vanuatu
Five	Afghanistan, Algeria, Antigua and Barbuda, Armenia, Austria, Azerbaijan, Bahamas, Bangladesh, Barbados, Benin, Bhutan, Bolivia, Botswana, Burkina Faso, Burundi, Cambodia, Cameroon, Canada, Cape Verde, Central African Republic, China, Comoros, Congo, Cuba, Cyprus, Djibouti, Dominica, Egypt, Equatorial Guinea, Ethiopia, Fiji, France, Gabon, Gambia, Grenada, Guinea, Guinea-Bissau, Guyana, India, Indonesia, Ireland, Italy, Ivory Coast, Jamaica, Kazakhstan, Kenya, Kyrgyzstan, Laos, Lesotho, Luxembourg, Malawi, Malaysia, Maldives, Mali, Malta, Mauritania, Mauritius, Monaco, Morocco, Mozambique, Myanmar, Namibia, Nicaragua, Nigeria, North Korea, Pakistan, Panama, Papua New Guinea, Paraguay, Peru, Russia, Rwanda, St Kitts and Nevis, St Lucia, St Vincent, Samoa, San Marino, Senegal, Seychelles, Sierra Leone, Singapore, South Africa, Suriname, Swaziland, Tajikistan, Tanzania, Timor-Leste, Togo, Tonga, Trinidad and Tobago, Tunisia, Turkmenistan, Uganda, United Arab Emirates, United Kingdom, Uruguay, Uzbekistan, Venezuela, Vietnam, Zambia, Zimbabwe
Six	Liberia, Sri Lanka, Sudan, Yemen

power...and right now, we have very little power over how the government spends trillions and trillions of our dollars...

Proposed Amendment:

Every federal employee must post all receipts on-line within 7 days with an explanation and justification of all expenses, or be terminated, unless the employee has been determined by a licensed physician to be incapacitated and unable to perform this task, in which case the expenditures shall be posted by the employee's immediate supervisor within 14 days, or the supervisor shall be terminated. The termination requirements in this amendment supersede all contracts of employment and all union agreements.

Longer Terms, Fewer Elections

America is the only nation on earth with federal representatives serving 2-year terms, which forces politicians to campaign *every other year*. ALL other nations on earth have more time between elections. Well, what are the possible benefits of longer terms? It cuts down the amount of time spent on re-election, and frees our "public servants" to serve We the People. As we all know, the President and Congress are afraid to make any waves during "an election year," as compared to the Senate, where they don't worry about re-election nearly as much. I suggest we try a three-year term for the House of Representatives, which would reduce campaigning by 33%, and see if it actually leads to more getting done. I know, they'll still worry about re-election, but not as much.

Proposed Amendment:

A Member of the House of Representatives shall have a three-year term. A Senator shall have a six-year term, with one-half of the Senate being elected every three years.

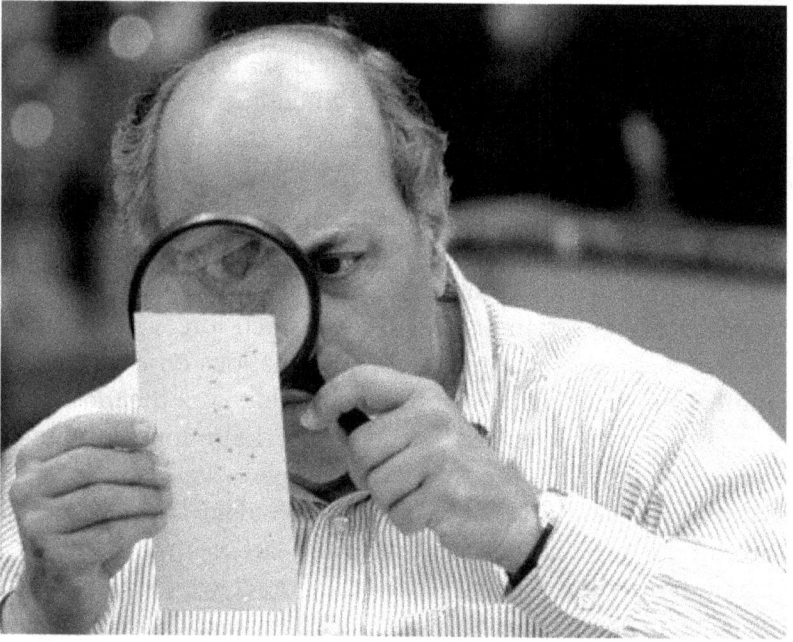

A Florida elections official counting votes in 2000.[68]

EQUAL PROCESS
FOR EQUAL VOTES

When I cast my vote, I like to think that it is counted using a standardized process without human interference, and that all American citizens have an equal say in who is elected. Unfortunately, as seen during the 2000 presidential election, there are many factors having nothing to do with your candidate of choice that can determine the outcome of an election, like ballot type, (re-)counting procedures, voter eligibility rules and candidate registration. In case you weren't around back then, Florida used a paper punch-card ballot, known as the "Butterfly Ballot," that was confusing, defective, and resulted in incorrectly cast ballots and a flawed re-count effort.[69] As a result, the Supreme Court intervened and, some would argue, ended up deciding the election. Of the 100,000,000 total votes cast, Bush won Florida and the Presidency by only 537.[70]

Now, I'm not trying to say that Bush or Gore should have won. On the contrary, our democracy survived a crisis that would have led to civil war in other countries, and both candidates should be commended for respecting a peaceful political process. (I worked for the Congressman from Palm

Florida's Ballots Were Confusing

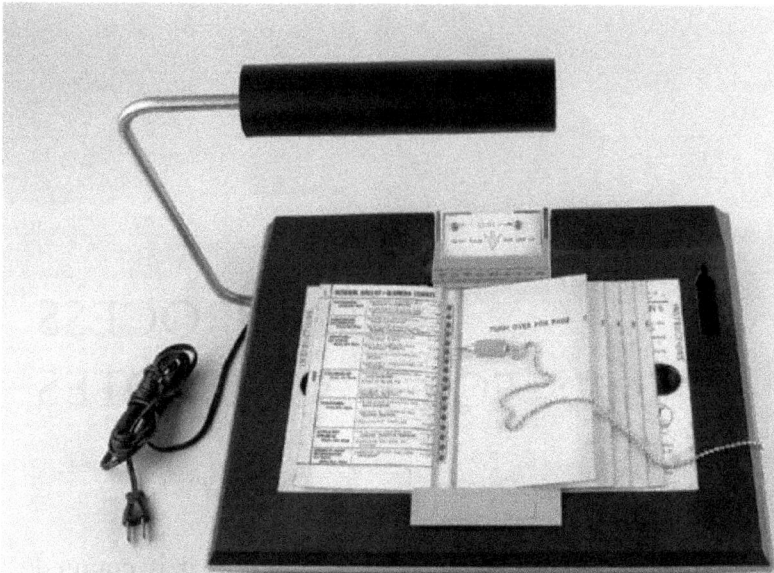

OFFICIAL BALLOT, GENERAL ELECTION
PALM BEACH COUNTY, FLORIDA
NOVEMBER 7, 2000

(REPUBLICAN)
GEORGE W. BUSH - PRESIDENT 3➤
DICK CHENEY - VICE PRESIDENT

(DEMOCRATIC)
AL GORE - PRESIDENT 5➤
JOE LIEBERMAN - VICE PRESIDENT

(LIBERTARIAN)
HARRY BROWNE - PRESIDENT 7➤
ART OLIVIER - VICE PRESIDENT

(GREEN)
RALPH NADER - PRESIDENT 9➤
WINONA LaDUKE - VICE PRESIDENT

(SOCIALIST WORKERS)
JAMES HARRIS - PRESIDENT 11➤
MARGARET TROWE - VICE PRESIDENT

(NATURAL LAW)
JOHN HAGELIN - PRESIDENT 13➤
NAT GOLDHABER - VICE PRESIDENT

OFFICIAL BALLOT, GENERAL ELECTION
PALM BEACH COUNTY, FLORIDA
NOVEMBER 7, 2000

(REFORM)
◄ 4   PAT BUCHANAN - PRESIDENT
EZOLA FOSTER - VICE PRESIDENT

(SOCIALIST)
◄ 6   DAVID McREYNOLDS - PRESIDENT
MARY CAL HOLLIS - VICE PRESIDENT

(CONSTITUTION)
◄ 8   HOWARD PHILLIPS - PRESIDENT
J. CURTIS FRAZIER - VICE PRESIDENT

(WORKERS WORLD)
◄ 10 MONICA MOOREHEAD - PRESIDENT
GLORIA La RIVA - VICE PRESIDENT

WRITE-IN CANDIDATE
To vote for a write-in candidate, follow the
directions on the long stub of your ballot card.

New York's Ballots Were Simple

Beach County, and heard my fill of stories about the re-count circus, from the political observers who smoked dope behind the dumpsters to the "independent" elections officials who ate chads that fell off ballots.) America did the best it could under the circumstances and the existing electoral rules. The point is those rules need fixing.

Even though the Supreme Court ended the recounts on the legitimate principle that each ballot should be treated the same way, and that differing standards denied citizens equal protection under the law, the Court did nothing to address any of the underlying flaws in the system going forward, including the most obvious lack of national uniformity.[71] MIT and Caltech have concluded that during the 2000 elections, 4 to 6 million votes were lost across the United States due to voting machine problems, ballot confusion, lost absentee votes and failed voter registration.[72] Well, if the electoral system was broken in 2000, and the Supreme Court or Congress never fixed the underlying problems, it seems we must do so on our own.

1.) Universal Right to Vote

This one is so obvious that I don't think it needs any explanation. Every American Citizen, whether by birth or naturalization, has an absolute and equal right to vote, but the Constitution doesn't say so...yet.

Proposed Amendment:

Every American citizen shall have the right to vote in all federal elections for Members of Congress, Senators and the President, and shall be eligible to vote upon turning 18.

2.) Standard Federal Elections (Registrations, Ballots and Voting Procedures)

If we have one federal government, then we should have one system for federal elections (the states can run their internal elections however they see fit). It makes absolutely no sense that states can set different ballot standards in federal elections, as opposed to using a uniform national ballot.

In Canada, our Neighbors to the North have created an "independent, non-partisan agency responsible for conducting federal elections and referendums." (Non-partisan means no political parties, while bi-partisan means two political parties.) It's called "Elections Canada," and is a model of perfection compared to our ramshackle patchwork of 50 inconsistent state systems.[73] Elections Canada has a nationwide ethical code of conduct, an internal audit service, and a network of local offices and polling stations to provide assistance to citizens who want to run for office, and to ensure that all votes are cast and counted according to the same standards throughout the nation. As you can see from the photo, no matter where you live, everyone votes by placing an "X" next to the candidate of choice, who is clearly identified by name and photo.

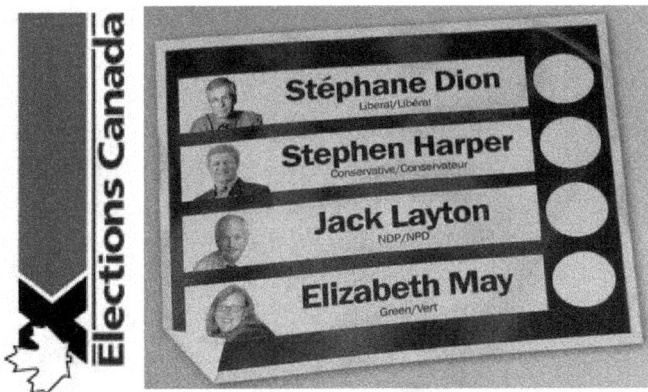

Oh, Canada, nice ballot!

In my estimation, the United States need their own independent group to standardize and streamline our federal voting system, and to protect each citizen's equal right to participate in our *self*-government. As our federal courts are charged with protecting the right to vote, I suggest we create a National Elections Commission as part of our federal judiciary, headed by a National Commissioner of Elections appointed by the Supreme Court. The Commission, as a *non*-political group, can establish a unified national standard without any involvement, influence or interference from our elected federal representatives.

And, here's a thought—we could create a partnership with the Postal Service, which already has offices in every community across the nation, and already has the address information for citizens who are eligible to vote. It would eliminate the need for polling locations that disrupt schools, libraries and churches, and it could share the cost of employees and office space. Maybe it could even help make the Post Office profitable!?![74]

These are some key areas where a federal standard would safeguard the right to vote...and help avoid future problems:

- Voter Registration: When I turned 18, just like millions of other Americans, I automatically received my draft-registration card from the federal government. The federal Social Security program also sends out automatic updates, as well as a Social Security card when you're born. Oh... and the IRS finds you, too, even when you're hiding from them in some foreign country. Why are voting *rights* treated differently? Whenever any citizen with a social security number turns 18, a Commission could send a voter registration card, to be returned to the Post Office, where the voter can get a valid photo ID.

- Ballot Creation: In addition to standard voter identification cards, a Commission could create a standard ballot for use across the entire United States in federal elections, whether it's a piece of paper, or computerized touch-screen.

Personally, I'd like to see ATM-like machines where you insert your voter ID card, have your thumbprint scanned, have your face recognized, and then you're allowed to cast your vote…at any Post Office in America.

- Voting Hours and Locations: Exercising our right to vote should be as convenient for as many people as possible, so why are some polls open for a single day in November from 6 am to 6 pm when most people have work and school? Canada has election periods, not election days, including four pre-election days over a long weekend: "Advance polls will be held on the 10th, 9th, 8th and 7th days before election day (a Friday, Saturday, Sunday and Monday)."[75] Canada's national elections commission opens its local offices where citizens can vote weeks before the elections by absentee ballot, too (which is why I personally like the idea of merging it with the Post Office).

- Candidate Registration: Different states have different rules for how a candidate for federal office is placed on the ballot, generally favoring nominees from the largest political parties. The Commission could establish standard eligibility rules without reference to party affiliation, and perform all necessary background checks. And, as candidates are applying for a job, the Commission could create a detailed application with questions about qualifications and employment history, and perform the research to ensure all answers are accurate before a candidate is allowed on the ballot. The Commission could also publish each candidate's information on a central website for voters to access.

- Campaign Contributions: If we are to streamline the campaign process (read the next chapter), we need a single organization to oversee and manage donations and expenditures. A non-political Commission could receive all contributions, manage candidate accounts, track the amount given by any particular donor, and ensure donors are American citizens, i.e. have voter identification cards.

- Campaign Expenditures: The Commission, in addition to tracking all donations, could also provide real-time reporting of all campaign expenditures, including the amounts spent on polling, private jets and advertising consultants, as well as coordinate all media purchasing, like advertisements on TV, billboards, radio and the Internet.
- Redistricting: Instead of state politicians, we could use computers, supervised by courts, to ensure fairness.

Proposed Amendment:

There shall be an independent and non-partisan National Elections Commission supervised by the Judiciary, and operated in partnership with the United States Postal Service. The Justices of the Supreme Court shall appoint a Commissioner of Elections every seven years or when a vacancy arises, who shall oversee and have authority over the operations of the National Elections Commission, and shall be responsible to provide registration of all American Citizens for all federal elections, an electoral identification system, and uniform nationwide balloting and polling, including absentee-balloting.

The first full week in [Month] shall be National Elections Week during which all federal elections will be conducted. The Commissioner of Elections shall operate balloting facilities for the entire week which shall include Saturday and Sunday. Absentee ballots shall be available for one month prior to National Elections Week. During elections, all polling stations must be open from 6 am until 9 pm.

3.) Update the Electoral College

Over the past 200 years, there have been over 700 proposals in Congress to reform or eliminate the Electoral College ("EC").[76] The EC is one of those things that doesn't really make common sense, and may even seem un-democratic, but when you step back and analyze its impact on how Presidents *campaign* for office, I believe it embodies the true spirit of democracy: to treat citizens not as numbers, but as people living across a vast nation, each with their own local issues and problems to face, and each deserving the attention of the country's CEO.

Because of the EC, smaller states like Wyoming receive a larger share of electoral votes than popular votes, which means candidates are more likely to campaign there, instead of skipping it for bigger states. Wyoming, with its 584,000 citizens, has one elector for every 195,000 people,[77] whereas New York's 19,746,000 citizens have one elector for every 680,000 people.[78] If the EC were eliminated, and elections were simply by popular vote, candidates could win by campaigning only in highly-populated areas. Under the EC candidates do not see 100,000,000 faceless "votes" across the nation; they see 3 Wyoming votes, and 29 New York votes, which forces candidates to account for the local situation of voters, instead of pure mob rule.

The problem with the EC, in my opinion, is that it does not go far enough in protecting the local situation of voters. In 48 States (except for Maine and Nebraska), 100% of the EC votes go to a single winner, which leaves many voters unrepresented. So, if you're a Republican in a Blue state, or a Democrat in a Red state, odds are presidential candidates won't be visiting you during campaign season. In Monroe County, a Republican area in Western New York State, voters are largely ignored by national candidates because the rest of New York votes Democrat. Same goes for southern Texas and northern Nevada. In Maine and Nebraska,

If we Changed Electoral Districts

Votes decided by entire State

Obama 332   **Romney 206**

Votes determined by Congressional District

Obama 262   **Romney 273**

however, they apportion their EC votes by the percentage of the popular vote—if it's 40% for candidate A, and 60% for candidate B, the EC votes are split 40/60 to ensure all 100% of the state's voters are represented. At the end of the day, isn't democracy about more people having their voice heard, instead of fewer? The EC already takes us part of the way toward that goal; I say let's take it a step farther.

If you review the maps on the previous page, you can see how the EC vote changes if it's by state, or by district. Now, I'm not saying we *must* switch to districts or adopt the Maine/Nebraska system…I'm just saying we should consider making the EC more relevant.

Proposed Amendment:

The President of the United States shall be the candidate who receives a plurality of votes in the highest number of Electoral Districts. The Electoral Districts shall be in equal number to the Members of the House of Representatives and the Senate, and the Districts shall correspond to the home districts of each and every Representative and Senator.

Convinced things need fixing?
Learn how to do it on page 107!

Ferdinand Marcos could not vote or donate to campaigns.[79]

AN ALL-AMERICAN
DEMOCRATIC PROCESS

There's a reason our Constitution begins "We the People of the United States"—because our democracy is composed entirely (and exclusively) of the citizens of the fifty states. Democracy is "members only," where citizens, and only citizens, are entitled to participate in government, including the right to vote. As a result, and as a matter of common sense, our election laws prohibit foreign influence in all aspects of our democratic process. To allow a non-citizen like brutal Filipino dictator Ferdinand Marcos to vote for the American president would violate the most fundamental tenet of democracy, or *self*-government. The same goes for financial contributions to political campaigns; our election laws prohibit foreign influence in that area, too.[80] That's why, for example, it was completely illegal for a 1984 presidential campaign to accept a briefcase of $10 million in cash from Mr. Marcos.[81] It seems pretty obvious, at least to this author, that if foreigners cannot vote, then they should not be allowed to use their wealth to influence our democratic process for their own interests, either.

Shouldn't this basic democratic principle, *Americans Only!*, prohibit interference from non-citizen corporations the same as non-citizen foreigners? It's obvious that corporations are not We the People, and therefore have no right to vote. Then why in the world do we allow these non-citizen corporations to participate in our *self*-government by donating millions to political campaigns? Under the law, for-profit corporations exist for one purpose, to generate profit, even if it means outsourcing jobs, or taking trillions of taxpayer dollars in bailouts after decades of mismanagement.[82] One would think the relentless pursuit of profit by international banks and corporations is just as foreign to We the People as the interests of any other non-citizen.

As for We the People who are part of this self-government, if our democracy is *Members Only!*, shouldn't all Members have an equal right to participate? Then why are the super-rich like Michael Bloomberg allowed to donate over $20,000,000 to campaigns, when 99.77% of us never contribute more than $200?[83] If each of us has an equal vote, then each of us should have an equal voice at election time, because democracy does not have a "high roller" table.

Finally, where does all that money go? To annoying and extremely unhelpful advertisements that are all show and no substance. In 2012, of the $2.1 billion raised, Obama and Romney spent a combined $896 million on TV commercials (88% spent on negative ads) that did absolutely nothing to address the real issues facing the United States.[84] That's $294 million *more* than the National Cancer Institute spent on breast cancer research during the same year.[85] Instead of wasting everyone's time and money on pointless "noise," I suggest we place realistic boundaries on campaign speech to force candidates to address real issues, which might also help eliminate money's overall role in our democratic process.

How did we get to the current system?
(This is a legal/technical discussion, so feel free to skip...)

When you sit back and think about it, campaigns and political speech are much different from, say, an encyclopedia, with one being part of the democratic process, and the other being part of the free exchange of ideas. Campaign materials are intended to influence you to do something, while the encyclopedia is just there to give you facts. That's why they call advertising strategies for Pepsi or Coca-Cola "campaigns."

The Bill of Rights isn't very specific in its word choice, and protects "freedom of speech" without distinguishing between the different types and purposes of "speech." Because the First Amendment says only that "speech" should be free, the Supreme Court has prohibited judges from considering the impact speech has on society, or the purpose of the speech (content-neutral), including political speech: "The degree to which speech is protected cannot turn on a legislative or judicial determination that particular speech is useful to the democratic process. The First Amendment does not contemplate such 'ad hoc balancing of relative social costs and benefits'."[86] Likewise, because speech is "free," the Supreme Court has prohibited all political contribution limits: "Congress may not regulate contributions simply to reduce the amount of money in politics, or to restrict the political participation of some in order to enhance the relative influence of others."[87]

This myopic view of "speech" as some free-for-all where anyone or anything can say as much as they want at election time is the root of many problems with modern political campaigns. Despite the Supreme Court's opinions quoted above, courts do in fact measure the social usefulness of different types of "speech," like commercials, novels, textbooks, prayer cards, hymnals, political campaigns, harassment, and racial slurs, and recognize that these different types of "speech" have different purposes, potential effects, and *limits*. If we separate the ideas of (1) free speech; (2) participating in the democratic process; and (3) applying (campaigning) for a job, then we *can* come to a different set of conclusions regarding the proper limits on each.

Truly "free" speech should apply only to "pure speech," or the exchange of ideas between citizens for the purpose of expressing beliefs or opinions on what is right, wrong, true or false without any intended personal financial benefit. Pure speech includes opinions, philosophy, literature, science, sports, food, arts, etc. The Supreme Court refers to this as the "exercise of the freedom of communicating information and disseminating opinion."[88] The theory is, if we let everyone talk about whatever they want, truth will make its way into the spotlight all on its own, kind of how people around town start to talk about a really great restaurant.

Pure speech is practically unlimited in the United States, and even includes statements of fact that are plain wrong. The textbook example is people who deny that the Holocaust occurred; those folks are wrong, and probably deranged, but the risk of preventing the "market place of ideas" from working its magic is too great to allow censorship (at least that's what we believe in America, including this author).[89]

On the opposite end of the speech spectrum are speech-acts, where your words are *actions* in and of themselves, and are not being used to convey a particular truth. This includes positive acts, like making a "Deal!" I don't say "Deal!" because I think it's a deal, I say it to enter into a contract. Speech-acts also include harassment and hate speech. All courts agree that this sort of speech is not "free." The law correctly prohibits me from following you around, yelling profanity and saying I want to see you and everyone like you exterminated. I cannot make a verbal contract to murder someone, swindle people out of lifetime savings, or play pranks that cause mass hysteria like yelling fire in a crowded theatre. This speech isn't for the "truth" of the thing being discussed, so the protections for the "marketplace of ideas" do not apply. Even the Supreme Court has allowed limits on this sort of "speech."[90]

Another type of speech is commercial speech—a mix of pure speech ("the facts") with opinions and subjective statements for the purpose of personal financial gain. Commercials are purely self-interested speech, intended to persuade the listener to give the speaker money. The fact that Tim Horton's coffee may be "delicious" or "America's favorite" (whatever that means) will have no bearing on the ability of truth to surface in the "marketplace of ideas." The law can and does limit commercial speech—no lies, no deception, and enforcement of warranties. Again, only pure speech is absolutely free.

Campaign speech is the most confusing type of speech, and includes aspects of pure speech, commercial speech, and speech acts. From the perspective of We the People, campaign speech is a "speech-act" by American citizens— the act of participating in self-government—which is necessary for a democracy to function. And, like commercial speech, campaigns incorporate aspects of pure speech (facts and opinions), but also include subjective promises with the ultimate goal of persuading the listener to do something to benefit the speaker, whether a candidate, political party, or voter. Well, if courts allow limits on speech acts and commercial speech, then why not campaign speech?

The problem with starting with the concept of "freedom" when analyzing speech is that you forget the impact the speech may have on the operation of the entire system. It is like telling someone to build a "fast" car without considering who will drive it, how they will drive it, or where they will drive it. When you realize that there are thousands of other drivers on the road, each with an equal right of use, and that other citizens cross these roads, your idea of "fast" changes dramatically, and you may even ask your local government to create a speed limit.

The same reasoning should apply to campaign speech. When you accept that campaign speech is part of the democratic process, you realize that it is not a free-for-all, but is a Members-Only operation where all citizens are entitled to equal participation. We not only can, but should limit "speech" that doesn't assist in the proper functioning of our democracy or contribute to the free exchange of ideas by (1) prohibiting non-citizens from participating; (2) giving all citizens an equal opportunity to be heard; and (3) replacing some of the useless noise during campaign season with meaningful discussion and debate over substantive issues. The following suggested amendments will replace all existing Supreme Court decisions regarding campaign speech under the First Amendment, and create a new foundation upon which future laws will be enacted and lawsuits decided.

I doubt George Washington would have used an "official campaign" necktie...or lipstick and botox.

1.) Eliminating Corporate Influence

Even though the Constitution begins "We the People," and even though the First Amendment is part of the Constitution, in 2010 the Supreme Court held the First Amendment gives non-citizen corporations the absolute right to influence our democratic process by contributing hundreds of millions of dollars to support politicians of their choosing.[91] Now, in my opinion, that's just plain bananas.

Take the Eastman Kodak Company, from my home town of Rochester. In the 1980s, while Kodak film was used around the world, the corporation had only one legal duty: to maximize profits for shareholders. So, while millions of dollars were rolling in, Kodak began outsourcing jobs in order to make even more profit. As a matter of law, Kodak had no responsibility to the tens of thousands of employees who were laid off during that time (from a high of 60,400 in 1982 to 2,300 in 2014), or to the families, friends and taxpayers who had to hold up the safety net for the thousands without jobs.[92] Instead, Kodak had a duty to make money.

When Kodak sought bankruptcy protection in 2012 (after years of mismanagement), the first thing management did was discontinue paying the health insurance premiums and pensions of retirees, completely ignoring the company's former promises to decades-long employees like Rick Diehl.[93] Kodak even showed them how to get Medicare and other benefits at taxpayer expense.[94] These were "legacy costs," according to then CEO Antonio Perez, which Kodak's new management was not obligated to continue paying: "I take full responsibility for all the decisions we've made to create a new company. I will not take responsibilities for the legacies bequeathed to the company by someone else."[95] (How sociopathic.) By eliminating pensions, Kodak was able to emerge from bankruptcy as a "viable" company. And, Perez received $6.71 million for doing it.[96]

How can anyone say that Kodak's interests are aligned with We the People when it comes to running this democracy? If Kodak cared about America, it would not have reneged on its pension promises and forced taxpayers to foot the bill, or supported endless free trade so that manufacturing jobs could be outsourced. Kodak (whose shareholders include foreigners) cares about tax breaks, not better schools for American citizens. The same goes for the auto manufacturers in Detroit, now known as the first ruins of the American Empire.[97] While the money was pouring in, Detroit and Rochester enjoyed high-paying jobs and robust economies, but as soon as the winds started blowing jobs overseas, corporations (and wealthy executives) followed the money and ignored the thousands of employees who helped build the corporations in the first place.

Why in the world do we let non-citizen corporations participate in our "members only" democracy? Don't get me wrong, I'm pro-capitalism, but I don't believe corporations should be allowed to use their money to influence our self-government for the single purpose of increasing profits. Here's a disturbing example: on Friday, June 1, 2012, President Obama raised $7.2 million at 6 fundraisers in

Moving to the Top

Honeywell's political action committee has become the top contributor to candidates this year. Amounts, in millions:

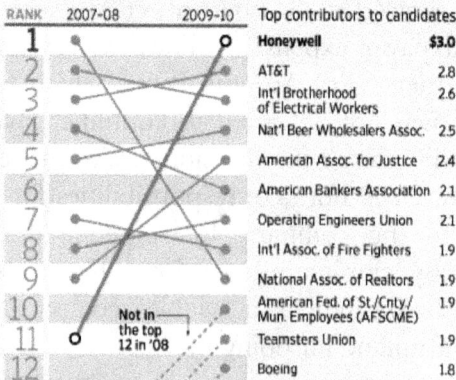

RANK	2007-08	2009-10	Top contributors to candidates	
1			Honeywell	$3.0
2			AT&T	2.8
3			Int'l Brotherhood of Electrical Workers	2.6
4			Nat'l Beer Wholesalers Assoc.	2.5
5			American Assoc. for Justice	2.4
6			American Bankers Association	2.1
7			Operating Engineers Union	2.1
8			Int'l Assoc. of Fire Fighters	1.9
9			National Assoc. of Realtors	1.9
10		Not in the top 12 in '08	American Fed. of St./Cnty./Mun. Employees (AFSCME)	1.9
11			Teamsters Union	1.9
12			Boeing	1.8

Note: Figures are through Aug. 31   Source: Center for Responsive Politics

Minneapolis and Chicago with tickets ranging in price from $50,000 and $40,000 to $5,000 and $2,500 per person.[98] And, taxpayer dollars paid for the trip, because it started at a Honeywell factory outside the Twin Cities. You don't have to be a rocket scientist to understand that these donors have Mr. Obama's ear...particularly the ones who are willing to spend $50,000 for a seat at a private roundtable event. The press, while reporting the "price-per-plate" on Mr. Obama's trip, forgot to mention that Honeywell Corporation, where he *started* his fundraising trip, was also a top political donor in the United States, having given $3,000,000 in Political Action Committee (PAC) contributions. The press also failed to mention that Obama calls Honeywell CEO David Cote one of his closest business advisors, and even appointed Cote to the President's deficit commission. And...the press certainly did not report that $13 billion in lucrative federal contracts were awarded to Honeywell from 2000-2010, all paid for with taxpayer dollars.[99] Banks and financial institutions are just the same, receiving bailouts in exchange for political contributions. According to Senator Elizabeth Warren (D-MA), CitiGroup helped draft the $1.1 trillion government spending bill to avert the bank-forced shut-down of 2014.[100] Unsurprisingly, in 2012, CitiGroup contributed $2,702,288 to candidates, including $491,249 to Mitt Romney *and* $209,452 to Barak Obama, and spent $5,520,000 in lobbying.[101] No matter how you cut it, corporations are not citizens, and like Ferdinand Marcos, corporations should not be allowed to spend millions to influence our self-government.

Proposed Amendment

Only American citizens registered to vote may influence elections through contributions to political parties or candidates, with all such contributions to be made under the supervision of the National Elections Commission.

2014 Top Organization Contributions to Federal Campaigns

Organization	Total Contributions	To Dems/Liberals	To Repub/Conservatives
Fahr LLC	$75,279,259	$75,279,259	$0
ActBlue	$68,026,527	$67,956,039	$33,675
Nat'l Education Association	$29,908,739	$29,072,307	$209,975
Bloomberg LP	$28,708,538	$10,692,165	$524,900
NextGen Climate Action	$24,574,615	$24,574,615	$0
Service Employees Int'l Union	$23,629,082	$23,489,082	$0
American Federation of Teachers	$19,689,548	$19,633,548	$51,000
Carpenters & Joiners Union	$17,308,189	$16,590,939	$717,250
Nat'l Association of Realtors	$14,976,234	$2,355,029	$2,549,050
Elliott Management	$14,199,672	$7,450	$14,192,222

Center for Responsive Politics (opensecrets.org): "Totals on this page reflect donations from employees of the organization, its PAC and in some cases its own treasury. These totals include all campaign contributions to federal candidates, parties, political action committees (including superPACs), federal 527 organizations, and Carey committees."

2014 Top Individual Contributors to Federal Campaigns

Contributor	Total Contributions	To Dems/Liberals	To Repub/Conservatives
Steyer, Thomas F. & Kathryn Ann Fahr LLC/Tom Steyer San Francisco, CA	$75,424,834	$75,422,334	$0
Bloomberg, Michael R. New York, NY	$28,549,392	$10,527,600	$515,200
Singer, Paul New York, NY	$11,518,474	$0	$11,516,974
Mercer, Robert L. & Diana East Setauket, NY	$9,676,399	$0	$9,666,399
Eychaner, Fred Chicago, IL	$9,669,400	$9,264,400	$250,000
Ricketts, John J. & Marlene M. Omaha, NE	$8,987,721	$0	$8,987,721
Adelson, Sheldon G. & Miriam O. Las Vegas Sands/Adelson Drug Clinic Las Vegas, NV	$6,059,236	$0	$6,029,636

Center for Responsive Politics (opensecrets.org): "Here are the individuals who have dipped deepest into their own pockets for campaign contributions to federal candidates, parties, political action committees, 527 organizations, and Carey committees."

2.) Eliminating the "High Roller" Table

Where I live, every Town Board meeting begins with "public input." Residents can line up, and everyone is given three (3) minutes to say whatever is on their mind. It doesn't matter if you're rich or poor, all citizens are treated equally—three minutes and nothing more. And, no profanity.

All American citizens should have a seat at the table of our self-government. But, our campaign laws allow the ultra-rich to use their money to gain a louder voice than the rest of We the People. Again, as of August 2015, 50% of all political donations to the 2016 presidential campaigns were made by fewer than 400 of America's wealthiest families.[102] And, as explained above, our election laws allow individuals to spend $50,000 for a chance to eat with our president. Just as with Congress and the President, unless and until there are limits on this sort of "speech," human beings will use whatever legal tools they have to benefit themselves and see their candidates of choice win.

While the Supreme Court has ruled that there can be no caps on the number of political donations,[103] Congress has managed to put "limits" on the amount a donor can give any one candidate or political party each election cycle. Following passage of the bailout bill (drafted with the help of Citibank[104]), which increased personal contributions to national political parties from $32,400 to $324,000,[105] the current "limits" are as follows:

- $2,600 per candidate or committee per election;
- $324,000 to national party committees each calendar year;
- $10,000 to state, district & local party committees;
- $5,000 to any other PACs.[106]

When these "limits" are repeated for 435 Representatives, 100 Senators, and unlimited Political Action Committees, it results in the super-rich donating *millions* in one election cycle (see the charts on the previous two pages).

Of 140,000,000 American taxpayers, the median (middle) household income is $51,939.[107] We have 15.1% of Americans living below the poverty line of $23,550 (21,140,000 people),[108] and 0.1% of American households making over $1 million each year (235,000 people).[109] So, why are the contribution "limits" set so high that 99.9% of Americans are unable to reach them? Does it make sense to base our system on what is impossible for 139,765,000 Americans? Does it make sense to allow any one person to contribute $75,000,000 when 139,594,000 don't even contribute $200? I think not. I think our system, in addition to allowing foreign influence by non-citizen corporations, is skewed in favor of the rich, and does not give every American citizen an equal voice along with an equal vote.

No offense to Michael Bloomberg,[110] but it is unfair (and unjust) that someone with an equal vote can apparently contribute $28 million personally and through Bloomberg LP to buy hundreds of campaign commercials, billboards and other advertisements to support Mr. Bloomberg's personal choices.[111] When the $28 million is compared with the amount I gave last year, it's pretty obvious that Mr. Bloomberg's wealth gives him a larger say in how we Americans rule ourselves. Self-government is the business of every American, not just those rich enough to buy campaign ads. Again...democracy does not have a high-roller table. In addition to it being offensive to the idea of self-government, it's given us the terrible political system we have today.

So, what is a reasonable contribution limit? If we try to create a system that gives as many citizens an equal voice come election time, then I propose that we limit annual individual contributions to 5% of the poverty line ($1,177.50 in 2014), regardless of the number of candidates and parties the contributor wants to support, at least on the federal level.

Proposed Amendment:

Only American Citizens with the Right to Vote shall be permitted to participate in campaigns to elect members of the federal and state governments, including participation through financial contributions. The absolute limit of financial contributions to be made by any American Citizen during a calendar year is 5% of the American poverty line, and such financial contributions are permitted only to individual candidates or to political parties. No candidate for office is permitted to contribute more than this limit to the candidate's own campaign or party.

3.) Eliminating all the "Noise" at Election Time

When politicians campaign, they are applying for a job. We the People are the management, and are responsible for hiring the best candidate for the position. So how do we make campaigns more like job interviews, and less like American Idol? How do we force candidates to provide thorough and articulate positions, instead of the typical empty promises? How do we minimize the barrage of political "speech" on TV, the internet and fliers in your mailbox (along with ads for used cars and groceries), and move past the empty promises without any objective and thorough analysis? (I love the ads saying a candidate will "Strengthen Families" and "Fight for our Community"— what in the world does that mean???)

Candidates will never stop campaigning. Every minute a politician spends campaigning, in theory, increases the chances of re-election. And, we need campaigns for our democracy to function. But, every minute a politician spends campaigning is a minute spent not working for We the People. I've yet to see a commercial or flyer that did anything to help We the People identify the best person for the job.

If campaign speech is for a purpose—to help We the People run our self-government—then we should lay some ground rules to enhance the usefulness of all this noise. That's why debates have rules, to maintain order and allow the focus to remain on substantive issues.

While TV commercials and advertisements start earlier and earlier every election, it has not resulted in better public servants. Why not limit some of this hot air? A shorter campaign season and later primaries will help eliminate the unnecessary chatter that makes many of us just turn the whole nonsense off. Besides, do we really want our leaders to be selected by 30-second ads with pithy slogans and superficial images the same as soft drinks and adult diapers?

Second, instead of relying on commercials and mailings carefully designed by advertising experts, let's require a large number of debates/open forums, and require the major TV, radio, cable, satellite and internet networks to broadcast them. If we want the best candidates, we need to institute a more rigorous application process. Today's debates are superficial, covering a range of issues with only minutes to respond, which allows candidates to avoid giving substantive answers. My ideal debate would be as follows: two candidates, two hours, and two short questions, like "What is your plan to reduce our dependence on foreign oil?" or "How do we fix our public schools?", with 30 minutes to answer, 20 for the opponent to respond, and 10 minutes to reply. With only one question, and 30 minutes to provide a coherent answer, a candidate must know a lot about everything. And, to spice it up, the moderator could interrupt with follow-up questions, and to spot problems or contradictions. It's like a law school exam combined with an appellate court argument. Only the strong will survive...and we want strong leaders, don't we?

Third, Members of Congress shouldn't be allowed to use taxpayer dollars to send "newsletters" to the district free of charge ($45 million spent on postage from 2010-2011).[112]

Newsletters full of photos of American flags and stories about bringing home the bacon are just campaign ads at taxpayer expense—not the legitimate business of government. Let's eliminate the use of free printing and postage to help a "public servant's" re-election chances.

Finally, it's embarrassing that America spends more than $6 billion (in 2012[113]) on campaigns that produce mostly mediocre candidates backed by the same special interests. I say we limit the total amount a campaign can spend. Of course, the devil's in the details, but here's a general proposal for us to debate over the next decade.

Proposed Amendment:

Candidates for federal Elected Office and any Political Parties are permitted to engage in campaigning with the following limitations:

1. No campaigns shall commence earlier than 45 days before an election to the House, 60 days to the Senate, and 90 days before an election for President.
2. Every candidate shall register with the National Election Commission, and shall be eligible to register upon procuring verified signatures from American citizens with the Right to Vote in the amount of at least 0.1% of the particular electorate.
3. Each candidate must complete a series of questions determined by the National Election Commission on general policy areas and plans if elected, to be published for all voters, as part of the registration process.
4. For elections to the House of Representatives, candidates may spend no more than $250,000, whether through individual campaigns or political parties. For elections to the Senate, limits are $2,500,000. For President, the limits are $25,000,000. (To be adjusted for inflation.)
5. All candidates for the House of Representatives must participate in at least four (4) separate televised public

debates lasting one hour for each candidate, but at least four (4) hours with one fifteen-minute break, with one debate to occur each week immediately preceding an election. Candidates for the Senate must participate in four (4) public televised debates lasting two hours for each candidate, but at least six (6) hours with two fifteen-minute breaks, with one debate to occur each of the first four (4) weeks following commencement of the campaign period. Candidates for the Presidency must participate in four (4) debates lasting two hours for each candidate, but not more than eight (8) hours with three fifteen-minute breaks, with one debate to occur every other week following commencement of campaign period.

6. Each debate shall consist of open discussion among candidates in response to one-minute questions from the physical audience, to be selected by lottery system. Each question shall be followed by 14 minutes of discussion by the candidates.

7. Each television network shall provide prime-time coverage of all debates under this section in the relevant geographic area, as shall any cable or satellite provider.

8. All candidates must provide real-time reporting of all expenses to the Federal Election Commission, which will be made public the following business day.[114]

Where is everybody? Probably out campaigning...

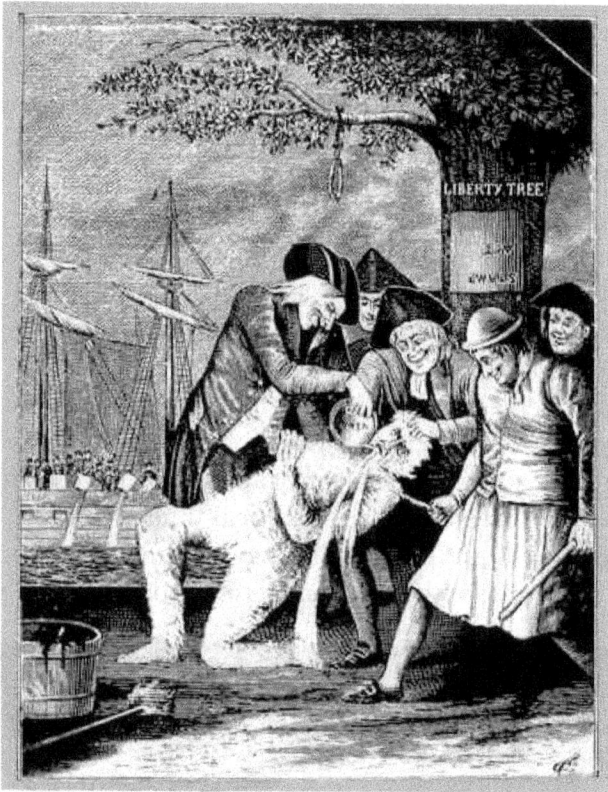

The tarring and feathering of a Colonial tax collector.

USING TAXES TO
CURB GOV'T SPENDING

Our current income tax system is entirely arbitrary, or, as my Cousin Vinnie would say, a "crazy make-em-up." That's because tax rules aren't found in the laws of physics or nature—they're developed entirely in people's heads. Governments needed a process for collecting money to operate, and so they invented concepts like tax rates, taxable income, qualified write-offs, and all the rest of it, and called it "taxes."

Because taxation was made up by humans, it can be used by humans for different purposes. Just consider the myriad of tax credits available to encourage certain behaviors, like buying a house or a hybrid car or a college education. It wasn't even until 1913 that direct personal income taxes were constitutional, and it was the Congress (not the People) who proposed the 16th Amendment authorizing it. Before then, 90% of taxes came from the sale of tobacco and alcohol (Congress proposed Prohibition, too).[115] Congress also has the power to distribute the tax burden however they see fit: in 1944, during World War II, the highest rate was 94% for income over $2.8 million.[116]

Current Progressive Tax

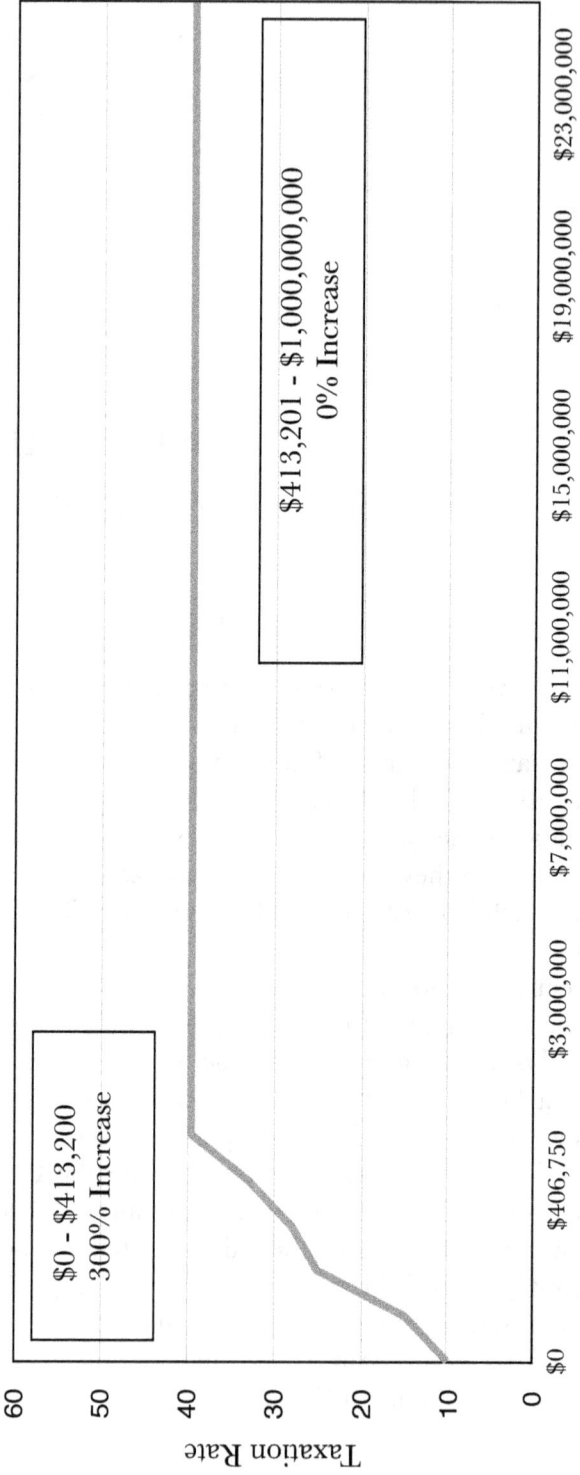

Taxation Rate

$0 - $413,200
300% Increase

$413,201 - $1,000,000,000
0% Increase

$0 $406,750 $3,000,000 $7,000,000 $11,000,000 $15,000,000 $19,000,000 $23,000,000

Well, if taxes are a made-up system, shouldn't we be asking if ours is the best possible? As you probably guessed, I think there is plenty of room for improvement, and that we can modify our personal income tax system to increase accountability for Congress and the President, strengthen a balanced budget amendment, minimize waste, and provide further protections against runaway spending and debt. I suggest a variable-progressive-flat income tax, which I think achieves these goals in a clean and simple manner, and provides the easiest and fairest method to make government accountable for what it spends and to tax every dollar the exact same way. Of course, I'm no economist (I did get an A in Federal Taxation), so we'll need an expert, or a team of experts, to crunch the actual numbers and see how well this will work in the real world.

Variable:

The biggest problem with our tax code is that rates do not increase with government spending. When the President and Congress adopt larger budgets, the tax rates stay the same, and We the People don't really notice. The same goes for overspending and runaway debt: in 2014, the IRS collected $3 trillion in revenue, and the government spent $3.5 trillion. Instead of increasing taxes, the government simply borrowed, so none of us felt it in our wallets, or considered it at election time. Our non-variable tax code has allowed We the People to grow numb to $500 billion deficits, and similar increases in national debt.

The solution is simple: we need to link the tax rate directly to the balanced budget requirement, i.e. adopt a "variable" rate. When spending goes up, taxes should go up, too, so that We the People will better understand what our public servants are doing with our money, and can hold them accountable at election time. A long time ago, Congress used to keep balanced books—during World War I, the tax rate increased from 7% to 67%, which kept the budget balanced, and the politicians accountable. Unfortunately, the honor system has not worked with the current crop of politicians, which is why a constitutional amendment is necessary. If the tax rates increased and decreased every year based on the government's spending, you can bet your bottom dollar that there would be increased accountability for politicians, and that our public servants would endeavor to keep spending balanced and taxes low.

Assuming We the People can pass a balanced budget amendment, then it should be easy to link the tax rates to collect the exact amount in the budget (maybe a little more for a rainy day, averaged across three or five years' spending). If next year's budget goes up, next year's taxes go up, but if the budget stays the same, taxes stay the same. And, we can

Variable Progressive Flat Income Tax

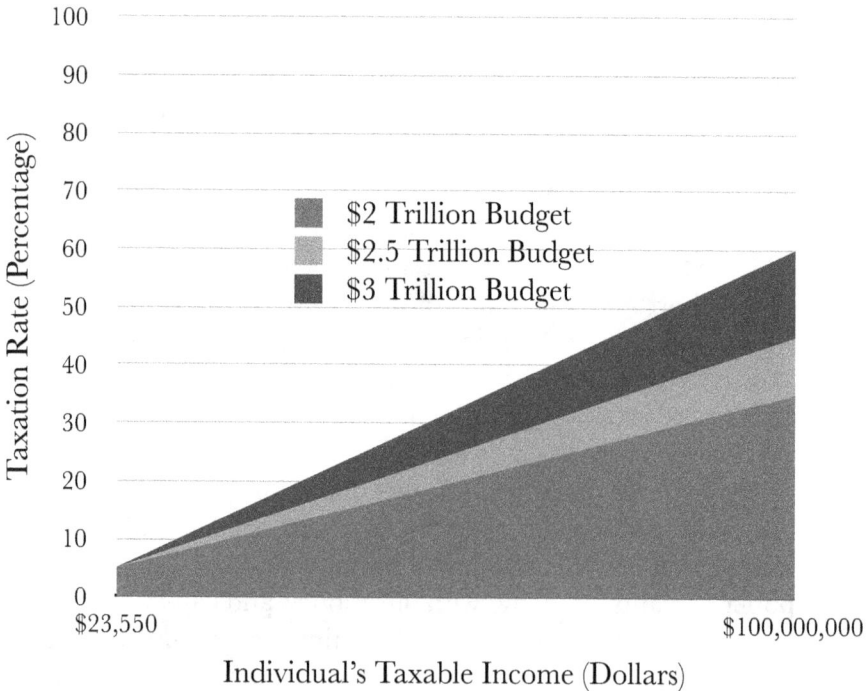

Legend:
- $2 Trillion Budget
- $2.5 Trillion Budget
- $3 Trillion Budget

y-axis: Taxation Rate (Percentage), 0 to 100
x-axis: Individual's Taxable Income (Dollars), $23,550 to $100,000,000

require Congress to set next year's tax rate when it passes the balanced budget by October 1, so we can compare tax rates to see how efficient the government has been with our money at election time in November.

Progressive-n-Flat:

The second and third problems with our tax system are that (*a*) it is extremely inefficient (costing $13,249,242,000 to operate the IRS every year, and billions more for accountants, tax software, and lawyers to sort through the labyrinth of rules and regulations[117]), and (*b*) it does not spread the tax burden evenly across all people. A "progressive-flat" tax is an easy and efficient way to implement variable rates, to minimize administrative costs, and to spread the burden evenly across all taxpayers. Many have urged the United States to adopt a flat tax, but, with all due respect, a basic 10% flat tax omits the variable aspect, which is key to curbing government power. And, it ignores a simple requirement of justice (one Warren Buffet urges[118])— that we are responsible to contribute what we can to the general welfare, each according to our abilities, not according to some made-up tax tables or human political agendas.

This is the only quasi-political issue raised in this book, because different political parties believe the tax code should achieve certain social goods. The notion of variable taxation is non-political, and I believe the following are as well, but I recognize that folks will disagree on this point.

The concept of a flat tax is relatively easy to understand. Instead of seven separate tax brackets with arbitrary rates and dollar amounts, the tax rate would be drawn using a straight line, like 10% across the board. In addition to eliminating the arbitrary nature of tax brackets, a flat tax would streamline the system by eliminating deductions, exclusions, loopholes and credits, minimize the need for the IRS, and free up $13 billion annually. (I recommend deductions for children and qualified dependents, and maybe charity donations, too, but the point is, keep it simple.) And, it would save taxpayers 6.1 billion hours a year in tax preparation time, and billions more in preparation costs.[119]

Beyond cost savings, a flat tax will minimize the possibility that the IRS can be used by the executive branch to target political opponents, like in 2013 when the IRS was denying requests for tax exempt status, and forcing audits and additional paperwork.[120] It's not as if the IRS is run particularly well: in April 2015 the IRS cut its customer service budget, and announced it would answer only 17 million of the 49 million calls received that year, with taxpayers waiting an average of 34.4 minutes compared with 18.7 minutes in 2014.[121] Now that's service!

While I believe that the tax rate should be distributed evenly, i.e. using a flat line, I also believe taxes should be progressive, where higher dollars are taxed at a higher rate than lower dollars (which is what our system already does, in a really messed up way). At first glance, people think progressive means unfair, but, in my estimation, progressive is a requirement of basic justice:

- "For unto whomsoever much is given, of him much shall be required," Jesus of Nazareth;
- "From each according to his ability," Karl Marx; and
- "With great power comes great responsibility," Uncle Ben, The Amazing Spider Man.

Our current system is progressive, so that higher amounts of income are taxed at higher rates, but the tax rate progresses 300% from $1 to $413,200, and then plateaus at 0% increase for income over $413,201. (Contrary to popular belief, there are no such thing as "tax brackets" where you are penalized for making more money: low dollars are taxed at a lower rate, and high dollars taxed at a higher rate.) I believe we should continue to tax higher dollars at higher rates, but it doesn't seem fair that the middle class suffers under a 300%

rate increase from $1 to $413,200 when there is 0% increase between $413,201 and $100 billion.

Imagine our current progressive system, except instead of a steep cliff increasing 300% from $1 to $413,200 followed by an infinite plateau, let's make it a "flat" line from $0 to the highest income level, with no arbitrary steps at all. How high the "flat" line rises depends on the variable amount of the balanced budget. (See chart on page 80.) A progressive-flat tax will allow rich and poor alike to pay the same tax rate on each dollar. And, all rates are calculated using a single mathematic equation (see below). So, Warren Buffet will pay the same amount of income tax on his first $50,000 of income the same as any member of the middle class.

Calculating the "progressive-flat" rate based on the budget is actually pretty easy (for folks who are good at math). Think back when you learned how to turn fractions and ratios into points on a graph, and how to do X,Y coordinates (rise over run). Applied to taxes, the rate of increase would be a tiny tiny tiny fraction that applies to every single dollar the exact same way across the income spectrum. So, for Congress to pass a balanced budget, it would simply set the rise over run high enough to generate revenue to cover all expenses, like 1% : $1,000,000.

It may seem "unfair" that the super-rich will pay a higher percentage of tax on their 100 millionth dollar, or like there is a "penalty" for making money, but that view misses the forest for the trees. On the contrary, our current 300% increase that plateaus after $413,200 is "unfair" because it *favors* the rich by avoiding the same rate increases on higher dollars that are imposed on lower dollars. I mean, why shouldn't the 300% rate increase apply to dollars over $413,200, the same as it does under that amount? A progressive-flat tax system treats every dollar earned the same way, using one mathematical calculation to determine the rate, based on how the variable flat line is drawn for that year. If taxes go up or down, they should go up or down at the same rate for everyone. It's an elegant way to implement variable taxes, and keep spending under control.

Proposed Amendment:

A Variable Progressive Flat Income Tax shall be applied to all Disposable Income (in excess of the Health and Human Services Poverty Thresholds[122]) earned by American Citizens and individuals earning income in America, and standard deductions shall be allowed only for qualified dependents. The amount of the Graduated Flat Income Tax shall be calculated based on the Congressional Budget and actual Expenses, with a proportional distribution (straight line) across all amounts of Income over the National Poverty Line, with a minimum rate of 5% and maximum rate of 75%.

2015 Income Tax Rates	
10%	$0 - $9,225
15%	$9,226 - $37,450
25%	$37,451 - $90,750
28%	$90,751- $189,300
33%	$189,301 - $411,500
35%	$411,501 - $413,200
39.6%	$413,201 - $2,000,000
39.6%	$2,000,000 - $3,000,000
39.6%	$3,000,000 - $4,000,000
39.6%	$4,000,000 - $5,000,000
39.6%	$5,000,000 - $6,000,000
39.6%	$6,000,000 - $7,000,000
39.6%	$7,000,000 - $8,000,000
39.6%	$8,000,000 - $9,000,000
39.6%	$9,000,000 - $10,000,000
39.6%	$10,000,000 - $99,999,999
39.6%	$100,000,000 - $999,999,999
39.6%	$1,000,000,000+

Historic Income Tax Rates (1913-2014)

Year	Brackets	Lowest	Highest	Top Income	Adj. 2014	
1913	7	1.00%	7.00%	$500,000	$11.86M	First Year
1917	21	2.00%	67.00%	$2,000,000	$33.86M	WWI
1925	23	1.50%	25.00%	$100,000	$1.34M	Post-WWI
1932	55	4.00%	63.00%	$1,000,000	$17.14M	Depression
1936	31	4.00%	79.00%	$5,000,000	$84.45M	-
1941	32	10.00%	81.00%	$5,000,000	$79.86M	WWII
1942	24	19.00%	88.00%	$200,000	$2.75M	Revenue Act of 1942
1944	24	23.00%	94.00%	$200,000	$2.88M	Income Tax Act of 1944
1946	24	20.00%	91.00%	$200,000	$2.41M	-
1964	26	16.00%	77.00%	$400,000	$3.03M	Vietnam War
1965	25	14.00%	70.00%	$200,000	$1.49M	Vietnam War
1981	16	14.00%	70.00%	$215,400	$563k	Regan Cuts
1982	14	12.00%	50.00%	$85,600	$211k	Regan Cuts
1987	5	11.00%	38.50%	$90,000	$186k	Regan Cuts
1988	2	15.00%	28.00%	$29,750	$59k	Regan Cuts
1991	3	15.00%	31.00%	$82,150	$142k	Omnibus Budget Act
1993	5	15.00%	39.60%	$250,000	$406k	Omnibus Budget Act
2003	6	10.00%	35.00%	$311,950	$398k	Iraq War Bush Cuts
2011	6	10.00%	35.00%	$379,150	$396	-
2013	7	10.00%	39.60%	$400,000	$403k	Relief Act

Hail to Me!

DIVIDE AND CONQUER

Our President manages 100% of the federal government at home and abroad, from the Department of State and all branches of the military to public schools, bridges, NASA, social security, health insurance, and the Post Office, as well as overseeing 2.6 million executive-branch employees.[123] Congress writes the rules, the Supreme Court resolves the difficult disputes, but the President is the CEO of America.

The Vice President, on the other hand, has no power at all, other than breaking a tie in the Senate, and balancing the party's ticket for election day. According to John Adams who served under President Washington, the V.P. is "the most insignificant office that ever the invention of man contrived or his imagination conceived." Or, as Vice President John Nance Garner said, "The vice-presidency isn't worth a pitcher of warm piss."[124]

The Office of the President deals with more than any one person can handle with the right amount of attention. The Office of the Vice President is little more than wasted talent, energy and resources. In my opinion, we need to ditch the Veep and divide the Office of President among two people: one to handle domestic affairs, and the other to handle international issues, judicial and diplomatic appointments, and the military. It's called a semi-presidential system, and it wasn't invented until 1891 in Chile.[125]

The Constitution doesn't say much about the Office of the President in Article II, but we do know that separation of powers and checks and balances are two fundamental principles within our current framework, intended to protect We the People against abuses by our public servants. A division of labor between dual executives seems the logical extension of these principles, and an easy way to increase productivity in the Executive Branch. And, as for the Vice President, we've already changed that office once by constitutional amendment, so maybe we can get it right this time.

When you see schools failing, bridges falling, our veterans denied services, and the Post Office going bust, it's obvious we need someone to pay better attention to things here at home. I suggest we create a National Secretary, to be appointed by the President and approved by Congress, to oversee the Cabinet and manage the federal government's day-to-day affairs, including the Executive Departments of Agriculture, Energy, Education, Veteran's Affairs, etc. The President, still quasi-popularly selected through the Electoral College, will continue to manage the military, the Departments of State and War (changed to Defense in 1947), all ambassadors, all federal appointments, and will travel around the world as our Head of State. By creating a National Secretary, we can eliminate a redundant office (V.P.), allow greater attention to domestic affairs, and adapt our Executive Branch to the realities of globalization in the 21st Century.

As an added bonus, if the National Secretary is approved by Congress, then Congress can "un-approve" a poorly performing Secretary between elections, including during a President's lame duck term. Our President, once elected, can be removed only by impeachment, which makes sense for the

Head of State. If the President does nothing to help our nation's day-to-day operations during a term, there is little We the People can do about it beyond waiting for the next election. A National Secretary, on the other hand, would serve upon confirmation by the Congress, meaning Congress can serve as an additional check and balance with a vote of no-confidence, and tell the President to appoint someone else who will do a better job (I suggest a supermajority of 60%). Of course, as the President appointed the National Secretary, the President also retains the right to ask this appointee for a letter of resignation, the same as any Member of the Cabinet, like the Secretary of Energy.

We wouldn't want this to devolve into a game of Rollerball, so we would need tight controls on when / how the National Secretary is appointed or removed from office. But, if we plan ahead, I believe we can re-form the Office of the Presidency into something more agile and responsive to the problems facing We the People and our massive federal government.

Germany, France, Portugal, Russia and twenty-three other nations have dual executives, and those governments have continued to operate just fine in the 21st Century.[126] In France, a President is head of state, democratically elected, and controls foreign policy, while a Prime Minister is selected by the legislature, and handles domestic affairs.[127] Russia has its own recipe for the executive branch, where a Prime Minister is appointed by the President, subject to legislative approval.[128] Political scientists have analyzed the different types of dual-executive (premier-presidential vs. president-parliamentary) for over 30 years, and we can draw on that research to figure out what's best for the United States.

Proposed Amendment

The Executive Branch shall consist of a President and National Secretary, whose powers and terms of office shall be determined as follows:

	President	National Secretary
Office	Head of State Commander in Chief	Head of Government
Selection	Elected by People	Appointed by President, Confirmed by Congress
Jurisdiction	Foreign Policy Military Treaties Judicial and Diplomatic Appointments Cabinet Appointments	Domestic Affairs Federal Agencies Post Office Department of Justice Veterans Affairs Banking and Finance
Residence	The White House	Naval Observatory
Term	5 Years	Until removed by President or Congress
Removal	Impeachment	Vote of No-Confidence by Congress (60%) or Recalled by President
Pardon	Eliminate Power	Eliminate Power
Succession	If dies, National Secretary becomes President, and appoints National Secretary, subject to Congressional approval	If dies, President appoints new National Secretary, subject to Congressional approval

Pardon Me...You're Fired!

The notion that the President can pardon criminals who were found guilty by a jury of We the People seems pretty undemocratic to me. There is a reason attorneys prosecuting criminal cases represent "The People"; because every crime, however "victimless," is an offense against our entire society (or so the legal theory goes). And, there's a reason the Jury are members of our community; because only the People have the power to adjudge guilt or innocence. Then, why in the world does our President have the ability to undo what the People have determined? That seems more royal than democratic...

On the flip side, if We the People have placed our trust in the President [or National Secretary] as the CEO of America, then the President should have the power to run the federal government however the President sees fit. I've handled a number of labor and employment cases, and, for better or worse, scores of government employees are allowed to keep their jobs after multiple infractions and demonstrations of gross incompetence because of various statutory or contractual rights. If the President has the fundamental authority to run our government, the President should have the absolute ability to terminate any government employee at any time (no discrimination), regardless of union contracts and grievance requirements. Our government is not a haven for the underperforming employee.

Proposed Amendment:

The Presidential pardon is hereby extinguished, and the President [or National Secretary] shall have the power to terminate any federal employee at any time, for any non-discriminatory purpose, as provided under Title VII of the Civil Rights Act, and notwithstanding the terms of any legislation or contractual agreement.

Hail to the Spouse?

As I'm sure you can tell, I don't like unnecessary spending, and in the United States, we spend millions on the *spouse* of our democratically elected President...yes, millions. Overall, we spend 240% more on the White House than the British taxpayers spend on the entire Royal Family ($1.4 billion compared to $57.8 million).[129] While I'm sure many of the expenses in Washington DC are legitimate, I have a real issue with the cost of the unelected spouse.

Here are some quick facts about our current First Family (it seems Mrs. Bush spent 212 days abroad during her husband's 8 years in office, which is more than Mrs. Obama, but I'm using Mrs. Obama as an example because the data is available...[130]):

- Mrs. Obama's 22-person staff costs taxpayers $1,591,200 annually[131];
- In June 2009, the taxpayers spent $424,142 for Mrs. Obama to fly to Africa (that's just the *flight*)[132];
- On March 12, 2015, Mr. and Mrs. Obama separately flew to Los Angeles to appear on TV shows the same day (Mr. Obama on Jimmy Kimmel Live to read "tweets," and Mrs. Obama on the Ellen Degeneres Show to dance to "Uptown Funk"), with the President's plane costing $206,337 per hour, and the unelected spouse's plane costing $28,334 per hour[133];
- Mrs. Obama's 2010 trip to Spain (why can't she find a vacation spot in the United States?) cost taxpayers $467,000[134];
- For the 2012 family vacation in Hawaii, it cost taxpayers $63,000 for Mrs. Obama to fly a couple of days earlier than the President,[135] and at least $100,000 to fly back a couple days later[136] (again, just flights); and

- In June 2015, Mrs. Obama and her daughters went on a "goodwill" trip through Europe (without the President) to promote her "Let's Move!" program[137] (to non-Americans), where she met Prince Harry and the Prime Minister of England, and attended a food fair in Milan with (the amazing) Mario Batali, costing an unknown amount, *plus* $127,781 for a quick stop in Venice to see the sights on the way back home.[138]

In my opinion, none of these expenses are justified. We did not elect the "First Spouse," and we certainly did not agree to spend millions in taxpayer dollars for the "First Spouse" to travel *outside* the United States. I find this waste offensive, and am shocked by the audacity of the First Family to live like royalty at the taxpayers' expense. Last time I checked, Americans hated royalty so much that they sacrificed their lives to be free...

Proposed Amendment:

(Add to Article II)

The President shall be given a stipend of $100,000 to operate an office and staff for the President's spouse, to be located within the White House, and with all expenditures itemized and publicly available on-line (adjusted for inflation).

The President's family shall receive protection by the Secret Service, including secure transportation anywhere within the District of Columbia. The President's spouse shall be authorized to use one Presidential motor vehicle for travel throughout the United States.

Today:

93% of Democrats Vote the Party Line.[139]

94% of Republican Vote the Party Line.[140]

February 15, 1798:

Congress Hall in Philadelphia

BREAKING THE
TWO-PARTY DEADLOCK

When George Washington was unanimously elected our first President, there were no political parties. By the time our next President John Adams was elected, there were exactly two, and those same two parties have been fighting over who gets to run things around here for the past two centuries. Sure, they have had different names, like Federalists and Anti-Federalists, or Republicans and Democrats, but from the inception of things, America has been in a constant state of internal battle where two sides fight tooth-and-nail under winner-take-all rules. This two-party battle has become so bad that since 1970 our system ceased to operate 17 separate times; because of strife between Republicans and Democrats, Washington DC has shut down an average of once every 30 months during my life.[141]

Season after season, election after election, and legislature after legislature, there is little progress, only this

"Red Today, Blue Tomorrow"
(Political Parties Aren't Set in Stone)

Abraham Lincoln's Republican States

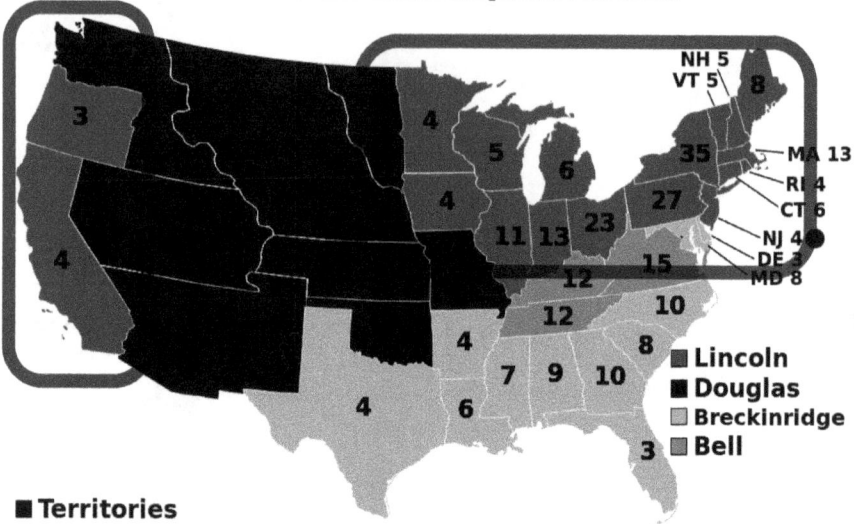

NH 5
VT 5
8
3
4
5
6
35
MA 13
4
27
RI 4
CT 6
11 13 23
NJ 4
15
DE 3
12
MD 8
12
10
4
8
7 9 10
Lincoln
4
6
Douglas
Breckinridge
3
Bell

■ Territories

Barak Obama's Democratic States

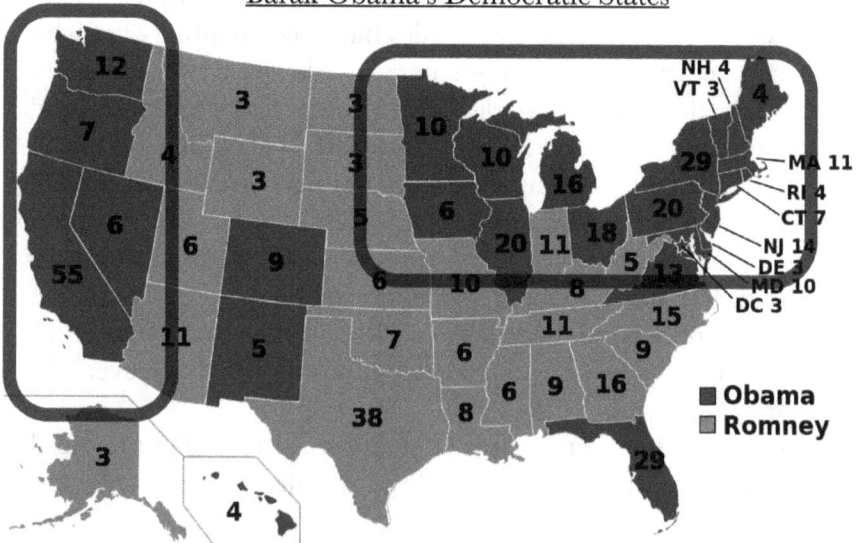

NH 4
VT 3
4
12
7
3
3
4
10
3
3
10
29
MA 11
16
RI 4
6
20
CT 7
5
20 11 18
NJ 14
55
6
9
5
13
DE 3
6
10
8
MD 10
11
DC 3
11
15
5
7
6
9
6 9 16
Obama
38
8
Romney
3
29
4

96

constant struggle, cheered on by citizens hoping their side will win. Sounds more like football than government. Having two sides makes sense in a game, where the point is to frustrate progress; otherwise, the game wouldn't be any fun. Two sides also make sense in a courtroom where facts are presented before a jury to decide a case. Politics, however, is not a game, nor a quest for truth: it's the process whereby people with different opinions work together to solve common problems.[142]

Beyond the fact that a two-party system is made to block progress, America is no longer a group of white men who see the world in one of two ways. Along political lines, a record 42% of Americans call themselves Independent,[143] which means almost half of Americans are not represented by the Democrats (31%) or Republicans (25%) in office, who are busy pandering to established party bases and donors to win re-election. Today's Americans come from all walks of life, and have many ways of seeing the world. We should all be represented in our own government, and we should (call me crazy) try to work together toward an actual solution for problems, instead of just chasing the next party victory.

There is nothing special about our two-party system of Republicans and Democrats. They are arbitrary classifications based on old-fashioned, pre-1819 voting rules (just like our single-executive system). As I learned in college, the Democrats of today are the Republicans of Abraham Lincoln's time.[144] Lincoln was a "Republican" elected by New York, Connecticut, Rhode Island, Illinois, New Jersey, Massachusetts, California and Oregon. In 2012, Obama was elected by "Democrats" in New York, Connecticut, Rhode Island, Illinois, New Jersey, Massachusetts, California and Oregon.[145]

The reason we have a two-party system is because of how we vote on election day: we cast one vote for one candidate to win one seat. According to political scientists like Gerald Gamm, a government with one-member districts,

Multi-Party Ballot (Invented 1819)

Official Ballot
Election for the United States House of Representatives
District One

You Have 2 Votes

District Vote	Party Vote
This vote decides who will be elected to the House of Representatives from this district. Vote by putting an "X" in the box immediately before the candidate you choose. Vote for only one candidate.	This vote decides the share of seats that each of the parties listed below will have in the House of Representatives. Vote by putting an "X" in the box immediately before the party you choose. Vote for only one party.
┌──── Vote Here	┌──── Vote Here

District Vote		Party Vote	
Fred Smith	Republican	Republican Party Kim, Dirks, Case, Packard, Deutsch	
Damon Washington	Democrat	Democratic Party Matteo, Myers, Lee, Bork, Gorr	
Cheryl Houston	New Party	The New Party Morkurski, Pine, Lebaro, Fletcher, Devino	
Naomi Lintz	US Taxpayers	US Taxpayers Daves, Chevalier, Brown, Noyes, Parker	
John Henderson	Independent		
Write In			

where the winner takes the district's only seat, will always be ruled by two parties. In fact, political scientists are so certain that single-member districts create two-party systems that they've named it a "law" after Maurice Duverger (Duverger's Law). So, in New York State, we have 27 Congressional Districts (of approximately 731,333 people), each electing one Member of Congress by the highest number of votes: 6 Republicans, 21 Democrats, and no third parties.

But wait! There's a new and improved voting method that allows for three or more parties, but it wasn't invented until 28 years after we adopted our Constitution by the Society for Literary and Scientific Improvement in Birmingham, England, and first used in Adelaide, Australia in 1840.[146] Under "proportional representation" rules, if we

98

add some "at large" seats for Congress, in addition to the individual districts in a state, and if ballots allowed two votes instead of one—one for a candidate and the other for a party —it would create a multi-party system. (Take a moment and look over the multi-party ballot on the previous page <—.) So, while I can vote for a specific candidate in my district, I can also vote for a political party to receive a proportional share of the "at large" seats across the entire state.

Almost every country in the world now uses proportional representation voting rules (see chart on next page), which allow third and fourth parties to emerge, causing parties to work together to reach the 50% mark for legislation to pass (yes, you still need a majority of votes in Congress for legislation to pass). If every American citizen had two votes at election time (candidate and party) as shown in the ballot by Professor Douglas J. Amy, Department of Politics, Mount Holyoke College,[147] instead of one, and we added some at-large candidates for each State (except Montana and Alaska, which both have one at-large representative already), we could eliminate the two-party hold on Congress. In New York, for example, instead of 27 Districts of 731,333 people, we could create 20 Districts of 987,3000 people, and add 7 at-large seats for the entire State. At election time, you can still vote for your personal representative, but there's also room for third-parties to win the at-large seats. So, if the George Washington Party receives 10% of the statewide Party Vote, but does not win any specific district, the George Washington Party will receive its proportionate share of the at-large seats—specifically, 2 or 3 seats. Now, we have a mediator to break the deadlock in Congress.

After decades of political battle in Washington DC, I'd say it's time we gave the multi-party system a shot, and put a mediating factor into Congress to end the two-party war. Personally, I'd like to see a conservative-progressive in there (against excessive government & for equality, science, education, peace, and sustainability). Sometimes the third

Nation: Lower House	Seats	Parties
United States: House of Representatives	435	2
Chile: Cámara de Diputados	120	3
South Korea: National Assembly	300	3
Kenya: National Assembly	349	3
Canada: House of Commons	308	4
South Africa: National Assembly	400	4
Panama: Asamblea Nacional	71	4
Russia: Госуда́рственная ду́ма Gosudarstvennaya Duma	450	4
Australia: House of Representatives	150	4
Germany: Deutscher Bundestag	631	5
United Kingdom: House of Commons	650	5
Argentina: Cámara de Diputados	257	5
Romania: Camera Deputaților	401	5
Japan: 衆議院 Shūgiin	475	6
Portugal: Assembleia da República,	230	6
Spain: Congreso de los Diputados	350	6
France: Assemblée Nationale	577	7
Mexico: Cámara de Diputados	500	7
Poland: Sejm Rzeczypospolitej Polskiej	460	7
Croatia: Krvatski Sabor	151	9
Morocco: House of Representatives	395	9
Italy: Camera dei Deputati	630	10
Switzerland: Conseil National	200	11
Netherlands: Tweede Kamer der Staten-Generaal	150	12
Brazil Câmara dos Deputados do Brasil	513	12
Denmark: Folketinget	179	12
Israel: HaKnesset	120	13
India: Lok Sabha	545	13

party's votes will side with the Democrats, and other times the Republicans. And, if we adopt a dual-executive, the National Secretary would be more responsive to We the People, as more parties will be represented in the Congress.

This really is one of the most significant and important changes suggested in this book. The two-party system is crippling our federal government: there is no debate, there is no cooperation, there is no compromise, and there is absolutely no progress of any sort. This is a change we absolutely need.

Political scientists will have to assist with the specific language, but I propose something along the following lines:

<u>Proposed Amendment:</u>

For each State with three or more representatives to the House, the State's representatives shall be divided among District Representatives and At-Large Representatives at 2/3 and 1/3, respectively. Registered voters within each such State shall cast two votes (one for representatives, one for party) and the 1/3 At-Large Representatives will be allocated to ensure proportional representation of all political parties.

The Legislative and Procedural Rules requiring Majority Vote for any action are maintained, except where vote by Super Majority is required.

New York's Chief Judge Judith S. Kaye
has done great things after mandatory retirement.

REGULARLY
SCHEDULED JUSTICE

One of the things I dislike most about modern presidential elections is the speculation about a candidate's *potential* nominations to the Supreme Court *if* elected *and should* a current justice need replacing during the subsequent four years. First, it underscores the fact that our Supreme Court is increasingly political, which probably isn't good for We the People. Second, in most cases, this sort of speculation is a sideshow that distracts from the wider range of problems facing America.

For example, just two short weeks before the November 2004 election, while our nation was at war and fellow Americans were risking their lives on the other side of the globe, then 80-year-old Chief Justice of the United States William H. Rehnquist announced that he had thyroid cancer, and that his doctors had performed a tracheotomy.[148] In the final days of the Bush and Kerry campaigns, the media justifiably increased focus on the issue of appointments, and decreased its attention to the many other problems facing America…like the war in Iraq. When it comes to electing our president, shouldn't we keep all issues in the same perspective, and not have the apple-cart of our democracy, piled high with problems to consider, tipped off its balance in the final hours of decision?

Federal judges have a very important job, and, in order to ensure independence, they are appointed for life. Unlike elected judges, federal judges don't worry about upsetting the community and losing re-election, which gives them liberty to decide hard cases the right way. There's a reason JFK and RFK went to a federal judge for an order telling Governor Wallace to admit Vivian Malone and James Hood to the University of Alabama campus in Tuscaloosa. It's questionable whether a local judge in Wallace's State would have been as willing to undermine the Governor for some politician from Massachusetts.

Supreme Court Justices: Age at Retirement | DailyWrit.com | Friday, October 15, 2010

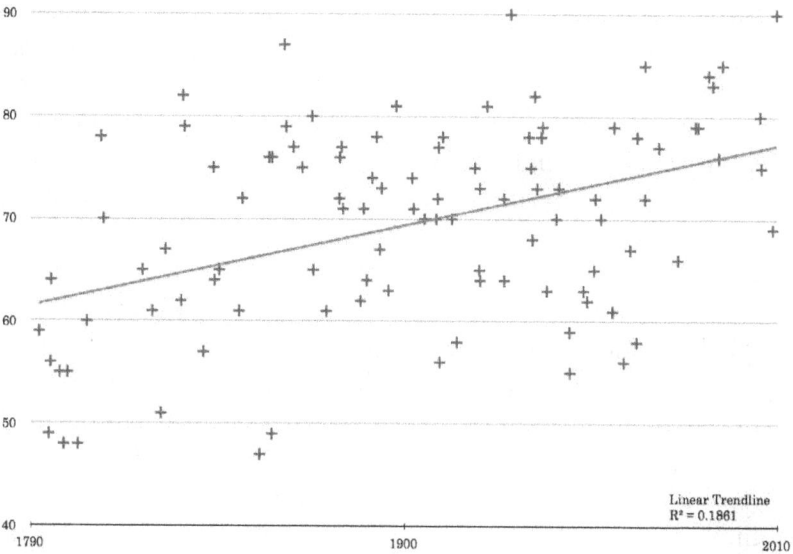

Linear Trendline
$R^2 = 0.1861$

Eliminating campaign speculation while ensuring judicial independence is easy: grant judges lifetime salary with mandatory retirement at 75 or after 20 years on the bench, whichever comes first. And, not simply for the Supreme Court, but for all federal judges. We have mandatory retirement for judges here in New York at 70-ish,[149] so when we choose a governor, we know which seats on the high court will be vacant during the next term.

Mandatory retirement also gives younger legal minds the opportunity to bring new energy and perspective to the constantly evolving issues facing our nation. Rehnquist, who was dying of cancer, continued in office during chemotherapy and radiation treatments, ultimately missing 44[150] of the 74[151] oral arguments for that term.[152] America is much bigger than any one person, and no public servant should ever be seen as irreplaceable, whether in Congress, the White House or Supreme Court. After retirement, as federal judges continue to receive full salaries, they are free to provide much-needed pro bono legal services; or, there is always service as mediators for mandatory alternative dispute resolution in district courts.

The only problem with mandatory retirement is the need for more judicial appointments by the President, and more confirmations by the Senate. During the 1980s, the Senate took 60 days to confirm judges; today, it takes an average of 223 days.[153] And, in the White House, the time from district vacancy to nomination has increased to 408 days in 2015 from 285 days in 2000.[154] We need functioning courts for a functioning democracy, and we must limit the time the President can wait to make a nomination, or the Senate can delay confirmation. I suggest limits on both branches: the President must nominate a replacement within 30 days, or else the Speaker of the House can make the nomination, and if the Senate does not vote on a nominee within 60 days, the judge is deemed confirmed.

As for the age limits, there are few human beings who get better at anything after the age of 75. It's sad, but it's also one of the facts of life. When you get older, things slow down; they don't speed up. And, as for mandatory retirement after 20 years on the bench, it will prevent politicians from avoiding the age limit by appointing younger judges, like John Roberts who was appointed Chief Justice of the United States of America when he was only 50 years old.[155]

Proposed Amendment: Mandatory Retirement

Federal judges shall be appointed for life, but shall be required to retire from the Bench after Twenty years or at the age of Seventy-Five, whichever comes first, and every judge will continue to receive full benefits through the remainder of his or her life. Federal judges sitting in a given court (District, Circuit or Supreme) at the time of this Amendment shall retire every other year beginning with the oldest until all Justices over Seventy-Five are retired.

Upon the vacancy of a federal judgeship, the President shall have 30 days to nominate a replacement; otherwise, the Speaker of the House of Representatives shall be responsible for nominating a replacement. Further, the Senate shall have 60 days upon receipt of a nomination to vote on confirmation.

PART TWO:

STEP-BY-STEP INSTRUCTIONS

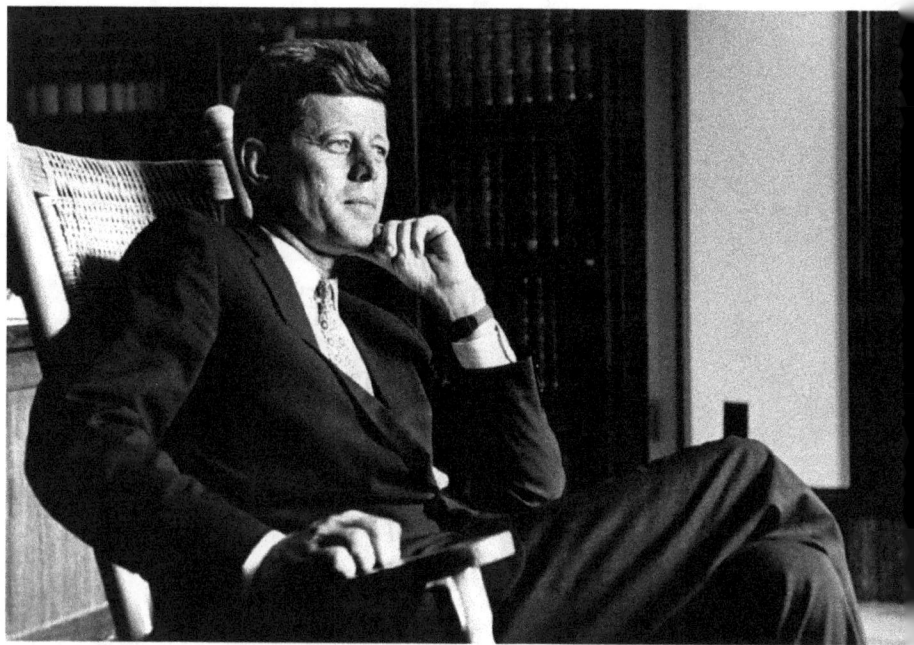

We are a great and strong country—perhaps the greatest and strongest in the history of the world. But greatness and strength are not our natural right. They are not gifts which are automatically ours forever. It took toil and courage and determination to build this country—and it will take those same qualities if we are to maintain it. For, although a country may stand still, history never stands still. Thus, if we do not soon begin to move forward again, we will inevitably be left behind. And I know that Americans today are tired of standing still—and that we do not intend to be left behind. But effort and courage are not enough without purpose and direction. For, as Socrates told us, "If a man does not know to what port he is sailing, no wind is favorable."

Sen. John F. Kennedy
September 17, 1960

State	House Districts	Senate Districts
Alabama	105	35
Alaska	40	20
Arizona	100	30
Arkansas	100	35
California	80	40
Colorado	65	35
Connecticut	151	36
Delaware	41	21
Florida	120	40
Georgia	180	56
Hawaii	51	25
Idaho	70	35
Illinois	118	59
Indiana	100	50
Iowa	100	50
Kansas	125	40
Kentucky	100	38
Louisiana	103	39
Maine	151	35
Maryland	141	47
Massachusetts	160	40
Michigan	110	38
Minnesota	134	67
Mississippi	122	52
Missouri	163	34

State	House Districts	Senate Districts
Montana	100	50
Nebraska	49	(Unicameral)
Nevada	42	21
New Hampshire	400	24
New Jersey	80	40
New Mexico	70	42
New York	150	63
North Carolina	120	50
North Dakota	94	47
Ohio	99	33
Oklahoma	101	48
Oregon	60	30
Pennsylvania	203	50
Rhode Island	75	38
South Carolina	124	46
South Dakota	70	35
Tennessee	99	33
Texas	150	31
Utah	75	29
Vermont	150	30
Virginia	100	40
Washington	98	49
West Virginia	100	34
Wisconsin	99	33
Wyoming	60	30

American teamwork.

WHAT WE CAN DO
FOR OUR COUNTRY

The true genius of this Project is the mechanism for action
—our vote in local elections.

It's free of charge.

It's easy to do; go in person, or fill out a form and mail it in.

It's our right, along with the time we need off work to do it.

And, it's not just something we're supposed to do, it's
something most of us want to do: we want to use the power
of our vote to put the federal government in its place. No
more debating with Washington DC, no more reasoning,
praying, letters, telephone calls, or petitions to the President
and Congress. All we have to do is vote, and <u>vote local</u>—
where our voices have the best chance to make a difference
and persuade our representatives to support an Article V
Convention. This is our opportunity to use the one power
the federal government can never take away from us—our
vote in state elections—to bring about real and lasting
change in Washington DC.

Changing the structure of our federal government is not some pie in the sky pipe dream; this is exactly what the Founders intended when they drafted, proposed and ratified the Constitution. And, it's not my idea; the peg-legged Mr. Morris and Friends came up with it over two centuries ago. The problem is that, while Article V is an awe-inspiring, amazingly democratic, and incredibly powerful tool unique among modern nations to control the balance of power between We the People and Washington DC, there is no instruction manual on how to use it…so here's a rough-and-ready roadmap for voters, legislators and delegates to use along the way.

The first step is to spread the word about Article V to your friends, family, and complete strangers. As the proverb goes, the people perish for lack of knowledge; until We the People know about Article V, there will be no Convention, and no change in DC. (I hope America's teachers will help spread the word—this is democracy in action; a living, breathing civics lesson.) The following pages contain some creative ways to get your message across.

Once citizens understand and appreciate the Article V process, we must persuade our state representatives to adopt and support resolutions calling for a Convention. We the People can lobby our local representatives with letters, emails, telephone calls, questions at debates, editorial pieces, meetings at the state capitol or district office with legislative staff, marches, demonstrations—and all this is in addition to the power of our votes at election time. If our "servants" don't obey us, vote 'em out. (Gathering information on all 7,421 state representatives will take some time, but if we coordinate our efforts, we can publish all the information on America2051.com, and citizens can cast a strategic vote for change.)

Third, our state representatives must propose, debate and adopt resolutions to initiate the Article V process and set the stage for a successful Convention. Finding one representative

STEPS ON THE ROAD TO CONVENTION:
1. START SPREADING THE NEWS
2. LOBBY OUR LOCAL REPRESENTATIVES
3. THE STATE LEGISLATIVE PROCESS
4. CONVENTION TIME!

---

in each state legislative chamber to introduce a resolution shouldn't be too difficult, but debating which limited amendments should be authorized, and identifying the ideal delegates might take some time. To maximize our chance for success, we will need hearings, studies, reports and recommendations, relying on and in partnership with experts, leaders and academics across all professions, industries and disciplines. (After two centuries, what's the rush? Slow and steady, fast and fragile.) The state legislatures are in the best position to handle the research and analysis; in fact, it's what we already pay them to do. And I would hope the 50 States will exchange ideas and findings, working together on the road to Convention.

Finally, we must convene and successfully run what will be America's *second* Constitutional Convention. Thankfully, this ain't our first rodeo, and we can follow many of the rules and procedures used by George Washington. Plus, there are constitutional scholars like Chris "the Godfather" Bopst who can help lead us along the way.

People have suggested that, instead of a grassroots movement, a new political party would be much easier, and would help focus the effort. That is the exact opposite of what I hope this Project will accomplish. We don't need any more dividing lines across the United States, and we don't need a massive national organization controlling issues and stifling debate. This Project is an information source and instruction manual with one simple agenda—change. Even though I've spent a lot of time on the proposed amendments, I don't care what we do, as long as we do something, and jumpstart the broken-down, rusting heap of our democratic system. Plus...no one person holds a monopoly on truth. The reason Part Three contains "fill-in-the-blank" documents is that Americans, not this author, should decide what the future holds for our nation and what issues and changes are in our best interests. As James Madison said of our Constitution: "This was not, like the fabled Goddess of Wisdom, the offspring of a single brain. It ought to be regarded as the work of many heads and many hands."[156] Americans from all walks of life must join together in a common purpose, realizing that we share an equal part in our self-government. We the People must look beyond our superficial differences and work toward a common goal—one at the heart of these United States—to form a *More Perfect Union* for all Americans

I realize the term "grassroots" has been manipulated by special interests and politicians as camouflage for top-down campaigns that promote a particular agenda, using propaganda pieces carefully designed by highly paid marketing experts trained to do one thing—sell a product. Thomas Paine had no marketing plan (or publisher) when he wrote Common Sense; he simply communicated a powerful idea that germinated in taverns, churches, meeting halls and homes across the nation until a true grassroots movement spread across the land, uniting We the People in purpose and action. That's my hope for this Project. Apart from this book, there will be minimal focus on any specific proposed amendments—especially online. For this Project to succeed, it will depend on you to make it happen. The question is simple: Are you committed to America's future, and willing to take action to see her continued success beyond your lifetime?

As I said at the outset, I think state legislators may have a hard time stomaching this. They could easily reason, if we're putting limits on Washington DC, isn't the state capitol next? And, I can understand those concerns. That's why I estimate twenty years to persuade the state legislatures to pass a meaningful resolutions calling for real amendments. It may require cooperation among generations, but we must be diligent until we achieve our goal—even if it means the removal of thousands of our current local representatives.

As for the special interests in Washington DC, if this Project really is *grassroots*, and millions and millions of Americans will build a network of action, then I do not see how any one group can peacefully derail us.

In 1776, many believed it was impossible for a few ramshackle colonists to defeat the British empire...but they did. Naysayers will always exist, and We the People cannot allow the defeatist mentality of narrow-minded folks (who likely have done nothing to help fix our nation) to hold us down, or prevent us from trying to achieve change. If we simply follow these steps, and vote strategically, we shall overcome. Let's get to it, America!

Step One: Start Spreading the News
Timeline: 2015 - 2020

It doesn't matter if you're an introvert or an extrovert, if you went to law school like me, or if you dropped out in the 8th grade to get a job to help the family like my Grandpa Paulino, there are plenty of direct and indirect ways you can tell your friends, family, acquaintances, enemies and complete strangers that We the People can fix Washington DC. When Thomas Paine published Common Sense, many people were ready for a revolution, but they needed the figurative lightning rod to motivate them to action. The message of Article V will have the same resonance for the millions of Americans who are ready to take control of a runaway government, but don't (yet) know where to start.

Without sounding too elementary, direct and indirect is a simple way to break down the tools available for spreading the news. Both are effective, both are easy, and if you keep your eyes and ears open, these opportunities are available every day. Think of the following pages as the "toolbox" for sharing the Good News with America! Use what you like, and ignore what you don't, realizing that your efforts are helping all of us build a better nation, now and for centuries into the future. The point here is to let all Americans know about the Article V process, to explain that it's our only legal and peaceful chance to fix Washington DC, and to help them appreciate that the first Americans *wanted* the states to update the Constitution from time to time. I mean, who can argue against the logic of George Washington?

Direct Communications:

You know people. You can tell them about this Project. You can tell them that if we vote a certain way for local representatives, we can fix Washington DC. If you do, I can almost guarantee that people will listen, because we all are looking for change, and we are looking *to do something* instead of making the same complaints.

So, what's the easiest way to bring up the topic, say, around the water cooler at work, the punch bowl at the church picnic, or the keg at the tailgate party? By responding to complaints about the current system, and the Congress, President or Supreme Court. The best part about this Project is that we have something to do beside complain—we have a legal and peaceful solution to our problems! Tell them the story of peg-legged Gouverneur Morris and the adoption of Article V, quote George Washington's views on amending the structure of the government, say there's a check-and-balance we've never tried, and let them know the date of the next local election...and who supports a Convention.

This book is another way to raise the topic. Lend copies to your friends or co-workers. Ask them what they think about all this (an easy way to engage someone is to ask *their* opinion). Leave a copy in the break room or on the kitchen table. Buy copies for gifts and just hand them out to people (all proceeds go to non-profit). Suggest this for your book club, or your social club, and have a discussion group.

Afraid of speaking to your friends and family, or worried that talk is cheap? Well, how about you write a letter, send a postcard, or include a flyer in your birthday or holiday cards? Or, go paperless, and email your aunts and uncles, post a message online, or text your co-workers with links to America2051.com. Drafts of these "direct" communications are in Part III and online, so all you need to do is decide where and when you'll spread the word.

Or, at the risk of sounding "old fashioned," you can always pick up the telephone and actually call someone...

Direct Tools	Indirect Tools
Telephone Calls	Convincing Leaders
Postcards	Conversation Starters
Social Media	(t-shirts, bumper stickers)
Conversations	Editorials and Press
Letters	Blog/Social Media Post
Gifts	Call-ins (TV / radio)
Clubs	Flyers / Bulletin Boards
Parties	Civics Teachers
Fourth-of-July Cards	Sponsor an Event
	(debates, panel discussions)
	Parades & Concerts
	Sit-ins, Marches, Picket Lines
	Tables at Festivals
	Advertisements
	Clubs/Meet-Ups
	Journals & Newsletters
	Write a Song
	Celebrity Endorsements
	Videos and Documentaries

Another idea is to throw a party. Invite your friends, have a good time, and take five minutes to: (1) explain why you love America, and what it has meant to you and your family; (2) explain why you support an Article V Convention, and the problems you hope to fix; and (3) identify your local representatives, and suggest that your guests vote for the candidate(s) who want a Convention. Folks have parties for things like candles, games and plastic containers, so why not have a party to support America's future? The America 2051 Home Party Kit basics are on page 169, and the entire Kit can be printed from the website, complete with invitations, menus, timeline, decor, (non) drinking games (pin the peg-leg on Gouverneur Morris), and some talking points and info cards to leave for guests (thanks to my sister Nicole the event-coordinator and brother-in-law Brian the chef).

The point here is you know people, and they probably will listen to you more than to a stranger, so get creative and make contact. Let your "network" know about the Project, understand that it's perfectly legal, realize it's a peaceful chance to make a difference, and appreciate that the States are supposed to update the Constitution and check the power of the federal government at least once every 200 years...

Indirect Communications:

After you've called, texted, sweet-talked, harassed, argued with, and eventually persuaded everyone you know, it's time to start telling *your fellow Americans* about Article V.

Indirect communications target everyone, but no one person in particular, including calls to a local radio or TV show, opinion pieces for the local paper, blog posts, flyers at the library or in elevators, writing a song, setting up a table at a festival, bumper stickers, t-shirts, pins, marching in a parade, or making a video or documentary. Just think of any opportunity you have to get on your soapbox and talk, like the public comment portion of your Town Board meeting, and go for it! (I do not recommend random introductions at the mall or supermarket or parking lot...) Scripts and draft editorials are provided in Part III, and online.

T-shirts, bumper stickers, flyers and buttons are great "conversation starters" with strangers and friends alike. You can make your own, (in fact you can copy and re-use any part of this book or the website for any purpose you'd like, except to make money). If you want to make t-shirts for yourself or to hand out, templates for iron-on transfers are on the website, or you can keep it simple and just buy them online through the not-for-profit organization (eventually). Same goes for lapel stickers. Or buy bumper stickers online. And...if they ask you what it's about, your answer is simple:

Good News! It's pretty clear that Washington DC won't fix itself, but, as it turns out, the Constitution has a 225-year-old check-and-balance that's never been used to remedy some of the biggest problems in Congress and the White House, like unlimited spending, corporate influence, and never-ending two-party battle. Under Article V of the Constitution, the States can call a Convention to change the rulebook for our federal government! And, there is no interference or involvement from Washington DC at all! The America 2051 Project is not a political party—it's a legal and peaceful plan for We the People to call a limited Constitutional Convention for the first time since 1787! All we need to do is elect local representatives in our State willing to pass a resolution saying they want to change the rules for Washington DC. Finally, instead of complaining, we've figured out a legal and peaceful solution, and we have the power for real change!

Indirect communications also include convincing community leaders, celebrities, newscasters, radio hosts, clergy, teachers, and anyone else with a following (even politicians) that the Article V Convention is the way to go, and then let that person reach his or her own network. Give them a copy of the book, and let them spread the word to the people you don't know. Have your celebrity cousin wear an America 2051 t-shirt on his TV show or on stage at a concert. Convince your old high school civics teacher or college professor or member of the local board of education to use the book for a class. And, when the family is gathered for the holidays, throw a bumper sticker on every car, truck, boat, bicycle, skateboard and walker you can find.

Community events are another form of indirect communication—and an effective one at that. Sponsor a talk by a teacher at the local library or community center. Sponsor a debate between the incumbent and the challengers regarding the Article V process. Not sure how to do that? Pick up the phone and call the library, or stop by and just ask if you could host an event to discuss the Article V process and to provide non-political information about your local politicians. Then post information about the event online, on flyers all over town, and in messages to newspapers, TV and radio hosts, and then invite everyone you know!

Associations, organizations, institutes, and groups of all kinds are yet another way to reach a broader "indirect" audience, by convincing leadership to support a Convention, or by writing an article in the member publication. Forming "clubs" to pool resources can help if you want to run some advertisements, sponsor a sports team, or host a lecture, panel discussion or debate. Get 50 people to join, charge $5 per month, and collect $3,000 per year. If I had a club, we would meet at a bar, spend about 5 minutes on business, drink, talk, and charge dues to cover the advertisements, sponsorships, flyers and public events. There are websites like Meetup.com where you can arrange get-togethers with like-minded people sharing a common interest. In Rochester, Meetup.com has groups with over 50 members for hiking, conscious capitalists, golfers, nature photography, indie films, bicycling, board games, hackers, bulldogs, running, skiing, meditation and UFOs. Why not a constitutional convention club that gathers funds to support the Project (or target local politicians who won't)?

For individuals who want to become involved locally, there is no limit to what people can accomplish if they are dedicated, organized and creative. I sit on my town's Zoning Board of Appeals, and I've seen first hand how complete strangers will work together against perceived harm to their way of life, like the proverbial cell tower directly behind the children's playground. Stop focusing on our differences, and realize that we're all the sons and daughters of liberty, and equal members in one great big diverse American family.

Making a Big Fuss:

When's the last time you bucked the system, and violated social norms for proper behavior? When's the last time you said, in the words of Howard Beale, you're mad as hell, and you're not going to take this anymore?!? If there's anything that gets folks angry, it's our federal government. This is your opportunity to let the world know about Article V and this Project. Pick up a megaphone, shout from your rooftop, wear a sandwich board, or paint it on your car's rear windshield: "WE CAN FIX WASHINGTON DC!"

I've seen rage in people's eyes when they talk about Congress and the President (which is one of the main reasons I wrote this), but then they bottle it all up, and go on with their every day lives feeling more and more helpless. Not any more, folks! Play some Bob Marley (he lived in Delaware for a while with his wife and mother[157]) about standing up for your rights, and *exercise* your civic muscles by taking a stand on an issue that really matters.

Politicians and
diapers must be
changed often, and
for the same reason.

- Mark Twain

Step Two: Lobby Our Local Representatives
Timeline: 2020-2040

After your fellow Americans learn about Article V, it's time to turn up the heat on our elected state representatives and *force* them to pass resolutions authorizing a Convention, or else we'll find new representatives at election time who will! We the People, by lobbying our state representatives *and* casting strategic votes, can make this happen.

So, what exactly is it that we want our state representatives to do? Well…these three things:

1. Local representatives must introduce resolutions calling for a convention in 99 state legislative chambers (Nebraska has only one);
2. Leadership in state legislative chambers must move the resolution to committees and the floor for analysis, hearings and debate; and
3. A majority of 34 state legislatures (67 or 68 legislative chambers) must adopt resolutions calling for a limited constitutional convention.

In this numbers game where every vote counts, the scale is tipped in our favor at the local level. Your state representatives come from your community, they eat at the same restaurants, shop at the same stores, have kids in local schools, and know the same people you know. Local representatives are also elected from smaller districts, and win or lose elections by smaller margins. In my hometown, there are 129,089 people in an Assembly district, 307,356 in a State Senate district, and 717,475 in a Congressional district. My state senator won in 2012 by only 5,448 votes,[158] while my Congresswoman won by 46,421.[159] And, in less populous states like New Hampshire, legislators represent only 3,300 people! So, if you pay any attention to your community, like reading the local newspaper or watching the local news, know the identity of your local representatives, and are registered to vote, then you have the tools necessary to call a Constitutional Convention.

Contact your Representative

Before we start voting representatives out of office, it's probably worth at least asking them to support a Convention. The same resources available for spreading the word to your fellow Americans will work on legislators, too. Write a letter, make a telephone call, picket a speech, or have a sit-in at the district office. As the proverb goes, you have not because you ask not—so our first task will be to ask our representatives to: (1) introduce or co-sponsor a Resolution; (2) take an active role in researching, investigating, and reporting on possible amendments; and (3) fight tooth-and-nail for the legislature to adopt the resolution calling for a convention. If that won't work, *then* we throw the bums out of office…

Organizing the Vote

Grassroots means this: 50 million Americans hear about Article V, look up their local representatives at America2051.com, persuade those reps to support an Article V Convention, or vote for someone new on election day. If We the People, armed with information about our local candidates, take action to bring about change in our separate communities, then together we will reform the entire nation.

But, before we can use our votes to force change, we need the info on the candidates and incumbents…and this is one of the things that could take a while to gather. The Project, either through paid staff or volunteers, is dedicated to obtaining and making all of this information public. Here's how:

1. Allow candidates and incumbents to submit their views on an Article V Convention to America 2051.com, including what issues they would propose for amendments, and whom they would select as delegates. (The hope is that, if the Project gains support among We the People, the candidates will be proactive in sharing their views);

2. If candidates won't volunteer the info, the Project will contact each and every one of the 7,421 current state representatives, and ask them whether or not they will support a Convention, using emails, telephone calls, letters, and good old fashioned face-to-face meetings.

Assuming our public servants do not volunteer their information, it would be convenient if Americans would reach out to their own representatives, get the info, and share it with the Project (email to candidates@America2051.com). If that won't work, perhaps the Press will step up and do the investigative journalism of days gone by…and print the information at election time. Or, perhaps college students could volunteer to contact local representatives. If all else fails, the Project will use proceeds (hopefully) from this book to hire folks for the investigative work.

What if the major parties won't support this, and only write-in or third-party candidates will call for a Convention? What if, in New York for instance, the Republicans and Democrats decide to sandbag the entire process? Well, then we move onto another state…or, we publicize the write-in candidates who are willing to support a Convention. (It's easy! When you get to the polling place, just ask one of the elections officials how to write in your vote!) One of the beauties of starting a new movement is its freedom from the powers that be, including the Democratic and Republican parties. Again, through the magic of the Internet, America2051.com will provide information on write-in candidates, and might even email info on your candidate of choice (hopefully). Ideally, the website will post information on "write-in" candidates who submit notarized signatures of around 0.1% of the district's population. The Project isn't about finding candidates to promote an agenda; it's about presenting voters with all options, and letting them choose for themselves what's best for their government.

As we turn up the heat at election time, we should ask more than whether or not a candidate supports a Convention; we should demand that they explain why they support it, and which proposed amendments they believe are needed to fix Washington DC. Debates, panel discussions and open forums are ideal tools to learn what a candidate really thinks, beyond the pithy slogans generated by campaign staff for postcards and TV ads. These events will also help us develop the issues on the road to Convention; having candidates debate discrete points and answer questions during campaigns will also enrich our collective thinking, and ensure that our representatives truly understand and are committed to change. In a perfect world, each candidate would answer several questions, such as:

- Do you support an Article V Convention? Why?
- Should it be a Limited Convention? Why?
- In what Limited areas would you allow delegates to propose amendments? For each, describe the problems to be solved, and your proposed amendments as solutions. Please cite all sources of data or information on which you rely.
- Whom would you recommend as Delegates? Why?

- How will you move the Resolution through your State Legislature's Committees?
- How will you move the Resolution to the Floor for debate and a vote?
- Who are the experts you know to ask for assistance in the following areas, and provide the qualifications for each:
  - Law
  - Economics
  - Taxation
  - Psychology
  - Procedures
  - Logistical Support

Local newspapers, TV and radio are ideal avenues for sharing candidate information—especially newspapers. Editorial staff generally have sway in a community, and can investigate and interview politicians more easily than members of the public. In my estimation, the American Press has an ethical obligation to report this sort of information anyway.

If all else fails, then the Project can take care of this (it will take time). If you're interested in volunteering, including contacting your local representatives and other candidates to determine if they will support a Convention, please email volunteer@America2051.com.

Once this information is available, and after the good news about Article V is widespread, it'll be up to the voters to take action and make this a reality. As this is a numbers game, the focus should be on the less populous states, where individual votes have the greatest chance to sway an election. Delaware, the Dakotas, Alaska, Vermont and Wyoming all have fewer than 1 million citizens, and smart ones at that! (Sorry California, New York, Pennsylvania, Texas, Florida and Illinois…but you're probably too big for your own good.)

Taking it to the Streets

Just because one lonely representative in the State Capitol introduces the resolution, or even dozens co-sponsor and support it, that does not mean it will ever see the light of day. It is up to the leadership, like the speaker of the house and whips, to move the resolution to a committee for debate, and to allow it to reach the floor for a vote. If the leadership won't support it, then the resolution could just sit and die with no action being taken…which would be a crying shame.

So, how do we lobby the leadership? Here are a few suggestions for how we can really flex our political muscles, and start the *bloodless* revolution:

- Sit-in at the leadership's district or state offices;
- March/picket line around the party headquarters;
- Start a boycott of the representative's day job (most state representatives are part-time legislators and part-time something else);
- Editorials and opinion pieces;
- Meetings with the legislator's staff;
- Heckle the representatives (boo! hiss!) at all sorts of public events, including speeches at local high schools, parades, committee meetings, legislative debates, and the representative's day job;
- Talk trash to constituents, letting them know their representative in leadership has to go; and
- Support challengers at election time.

Coordinating group events like marches and sit-ins is cheap and easy in the 21st Century using the magic of social media. Convincing legislative leaders to support a Convention will require coordination across individual states, and volunteers willing to pass petitions, send emails, organize events, and share information with Americans from all walks of life, but it will also provide a vitally needed opportunity for all of us to work together!

Lobbying legislative leadership is the first part of the Project that will require widespread coordination of feet-on-the-street. Most dialogue and debate will happen within the state's legislative districts, both at election time and during the year. As citizens unite over issues or candidates, groups will form, and they can publish their contact information online, too. Beyond the home districts, local volunteers could coordinate state-wide days to visit the capitol and schedule meetings, talks, demonstrations, or other events to influence party bosses to action. As May 14 was the first day of the Convention of 1787, I suppose we could head to all 50 state capitols May 14!

Sit-ins, picket lines, and heckling the legislative chamber, you say??? Now, call me crazy (or just mad), but I'm willing to go to jail or the grave to help fix the United States, just like countless other Americans through the years. Civil disobedience has helped us make progress in critical areas through the years—and that's about as grassroots as it gets. But…it's certainly not for everyone.

Rosa Parks remains an inspiration.

The sit-in is a powerful tool of non-violent protest.
(These Berkeley students successfully swarmed a police car
and stopped the arrest of the person on the car's roof.)

Political Action Toolbox

Writing letters and sending emails are easy enough, but what about things like sit-ins, petitions, and lobbying days at the state capitol? Plenty of groups have successfully lobbied our government in the past—this is nothing new. Here are some of the things I'd be willing to do for change.

Passing Petitions: In school, we used to pass petitions for just about everything, from extending the time for lunch to using a curve when grading a particularly hard test. It was an easy, non-confrontational way to let our teachers understand just how we felt. And, while the petition only said we supported some change, and never mentioned the consequences of inaction…our teachers had no problem understanding unhappy students are prone to misbehave.

Petitions are as simple as pie to design and circulate among your fellow citizens. They tell a person to do something, and demonstrate how many people want that thing to happen. Here's an example:

I Petition (REPRESENTATIVE or LEGISLATURE) to (TAKE ACTION), and swear/affirm that the following is my correct name, address, license number and signature:			
Name	Address	Identifier (License #)	Signature (dated)
Nicole			
Jimmy			
Rachel			
Zach			
Natalie			
Joey			

Complete yours in two easy steps: identify the intended recipient, like your current representative, or maybe the speaker, or the entire legislature, and then decide what you want that person/body to do. Just fill in the blanks! You can ask your representative to vote YES on a resolution, or you can ask the entire body to authorize a balanced budget amendment. Or, you could petition your local newspaper to support a particular person at election time. The opportunities are endless.

Be creative in obtaining signatures, looking beyond your friends, family and acquaintances to your fellow Americans from all walks of life. Keep a petition with you in your purse, gym bag, briefcase, fanny pack, knapsack, or anything else you carry, wear your America 2051 t-shirt, and ask everyone who makes eye contact to sign up. Set up a table at the mall, library or local park. (To keep people honest, I recommend including a personal identifier, like a driver's license number, which has nothing to do with your credit score, but that may be overkill.)

Peaceful Demonstrations: In the 21st Century, social media make it easy to gather and share information, as well as to coordinate action with complete strangers. Nowadays, you don't have to be Father Ted Hesburgh or Martin Luther King, Jr. to organize. If a brave American will create an on-line event, like a sit-in, picket line, flash-mob, or day to visit the state capitol, strangers can join and spread the word with a few taps on a phone or clicks on a computer.

A non-political example is the "flashmob" that shut down London's Liverpool Street train station at 7 pm on Wednesday, February 18, 2009.[160] For ten minutes, thousands of strangers poured into the train station, and precisely on the hour (ah...British punctuality) donned their earphones, turned on a specific song and started dancing. The "Liverpool Street Station Silent Dance" Facebook group was easily organized by a 22-year-old who invited his friends, who invited their friends, until thousands joined to reenact the dance number from a TV commercial. With practically no effort, 14,000 people joined the Facebook group, thousands showed up, danced, and left with no arrests.

More recently, in America the "Black [indeed, All] Lives Matter" movement has been making plenty of waves, with over 50 folks arrested outside a federal courthouse, and shutting down major highways.[161] In one week, thousands took to the streets in protest across the United States, shutting down I-35 outside of Dallas, a train station and I-580 in Oakland, I-75/85 outside Atlanta, and malls and roads outside St. Louis.[162] These were all non-violent events, where a small number of people garnered national attention for their cause in a generally peaceful manner.

Are you willing to take the day off of work, and sit down with 2,500 other people to block the street to the state capitol building? How about taking a 4-hour shift, two days a week, along with 25,000 other people keeping a constant presence outside the office of your public servant? Thanks to social media, if you already know thousands of people signed up online, I'm sure it'll be much easier for you to show up, too…

<u>Smartphone</u>: Not only are these mini-computers gateways to social media, they are also compact recording devices where you can gather information (and then share it over social media). Take a video of your current representative while you ask if they support the Convention process or a particular amendment. Post the video and forward it to local news and radio, as well as your friends, at election time...and let everyone know what you think about the answer. (Or, support a challenger, and broadcast their answers supporting a Convention.)

Don't be afraid to think low-tech, either. To make a YouTube video or TV commercial, take four pieces of paper, write one message on each, place them in order, and use your cell phone to take a video of the stack while you slowly pull sheets off to reveal the pages below:

1. "America needs its Constitution fixed."
2. "Candidate [NAME] refuses to do it (or to help)." (Feel free to tape on a photo.)
3. "Let's not re-elect Candidate [NAME]." (Feel free to tape on a photo.)
4. "Let's form a more perfect Union."

It's how they filmed the opening credits in *It's a Wonderful Life*, and plenty of other movies back in the day, and is enough to get your point across in a simple, concise manner.

<u>One-to-One Meetings</u>: I know plenty of people who have a lot to say, but are afraid of saying it to someone's face. If that's you, get over it. Your voice is important not because of the words you choose, but because of who you are—a voting citizen, with an equal say in what our government should be doing. Who cares if your elected representative wears a fancy suit and has a silver tongue. You're the boss, and they are the hired servants. If you're willing to meet with your representative, or the press, but...you don't know where to start, I suggest you keep it simple. Tell them what you think

and why you think it, then ask them if they will support your idea. It's a petition, only without the piece of paper.

National Organization: While I want this to be grassroots, the Project will be working in the background to keep everyone up-to-date on news and progress, sharing information on all candidates (while supporting none!), coordinating volunteers in 50 states, keeping a calendar of local events, and soliciting research, discussions, talks, and reports on the amendment ideas. But, I don't think any of this is needed if We the People will pitch in (there's a reason I've hidden this toward the end of the book...)

What is the Project? It's a non-profit organization, with a Board of Directors who oversee the money, and volunteers. All proceeds from the book and swag will hopefully pay any bills. The Project will be a central repository for all information about candidates, and about amendment issues. But, enough of that...back to We the People.

I-580 in Oakland, California on Monday, November 24, 2014

Part Three: The Legislative Process
Timeline: 2020-2040

The first milepost in the Project is to find local representatives across America to research, understand, and propose resolutions calling for a Convention. But, that's only the beginning, because those lonely representatives must also persuade their fellow legislators to do the same, and to participate in research, analysis, and plenty of debates over what amendments should be authorized for debate at the Convention.

Introducing the Resolution

The state resolution is the key needed to start the convention, and to legitimize its work in the eyes of our courts. Just like the deed to a house on record with the county clerk, our government runs on specific pieces of paper, including the state resolution. This particular legislative document is not complex, but it is important, and it defines the power the states are giving the convention to make changes. So…what must the resolution say? Four things:

    1. We are calling for a Convention,

2. The Convention is authorized to propose amendments to solve [THESE] specific problems—and nothing else;
3. We want [NAMES] to be our state's delegates; and
4. We want the Convention at a certain time and place.

Once a state legislature passes its resolution, its clerk will send a certified copy to the National Archivist in Washington, DC, who is a form of National Clerk to receive and record documents for the American people and federal government. The Archivist will then publish the Resolutions in the National Register and US Statutes at Large. When 34 resolutions are published by the Archivist, the Convention receives the legal authority to convene, to propose amendments to the Constitution, and to send the proposals to the states for ratification. Without these steps, courts will deem the Convention illegal.

It shouldn't be too difficult for We the People to find a mere 99 local representatives across these United States—one for each state legislative chamber—to complete the fill-in-the-blank resolution and sponsor's memorandum (pages 150-159), hand it to the legislature's clerk, and be a broken record for change

Research and Analysis (Subject Matter)

A fill-in-the-blank resolution is just a starting point, and over the next decade or so, state legislatures will debate the critical issue of what problems should be fixed, and which delegates should be sent to do it. It took 18 years for *medical* marijuana to pass in New York—politicians are afraid of change, and, at least in the Empire State, apparently know more about treating patients than duly licensed medical doctors.[163] This could take just as long.

State legislatures already have the procedures and resources available to oversee this sort of research through their current committees. After a bill or resolution is introduced, the speaker can send it to one of many committees for review and markup, each with its own subject matter jurisdiction. Missouri is an ideal example of a robust legislative committee structure—each with its own members and staff to assist with reviewing, researching, and reporting on bills:

1. Select Committee on State and Local Government;
2. Select Committee on Financial Institutions and Taxation;
3. Committee on Emerging Issues;
4. Select Committee on Budget;
5. Joint Committee on Tax Policy;
6. Committee on Fiscal Review;
7. Joint Committee on the Justice System;
8. Joint Committee on Legislative Research;
9. Joint Committee on Government Accountability;
10. Committee on Government Oversight;
11. Committee on Government Efficiency;
12. Committee on Elections; and
13. Committee on Civil and Criminal Proceedings.

Most states also have their own public education departments and university systems, too, which can assist in reviewing these issues and issuing reports.

Limited government resources are an obstacle, but We the People can fill the gap if leaders in business, science, industry, medicine, law, economics, and all other disciplines will conduct their own research and report their conclusions as to what amendments will and will not work. Before we can change budgeting and tax rules, we need economists to study the issue, and political scientists to analyze how it would impact the effectiveness of Congress based on historical precedent. The Project (as a non-profit) can assist in coordinating action and information through this stage. University symposia, where the experts in a field write papers and give presentations on a certain topic, are the perfect example of Americans helping the government (as opposed to universities waiting for federal grants before they do work...). At the University of Rochester, the business school and department of political science can easily partner in conducting significant research on these issues, and present it to all 50 state legislatures for consideration. Remember...this is our chance to work with all Americans, and not just those within our field or profession. Life does not evolve without cross-pollination.

Research and Analysis (Delegates)

As to *who* should serve as delegates, that can make or break the success of this Project. We will need delegates who can think independently, work together, duke it out with other really smart folks in the middle of nowhere for weeks on end, and maintain the secrecy of all proceedings. The ideal delegate will understand psychology, political science, law, international relations, organizational structure and efficiency, business and commerce, etc. And, they'll have to work together with 250+ other people to make America the best it can be. I think at the very least we might include each state's chief judge, or the judge's delegate. I also believe we *must* exclude all current and former public servants, elected or employed, serving at the state or federal level. That way, the governor or current members of state legislature or congress cannot be part of the Convention, or the employees who serve at their pleasure. And, as for the former elected officials, they shouldn't be considered either—they're the ones who got us into this mess in the first place.

When I think about the smartest people in my state, I think about academics, business and community leaders, doctors, scientists, clergy, and publishers, but generally not our elected representatives, or their high-level staff. And, even if your first thought was your local representative, odds are there are other people just as qualified who can handle this important work. I realize that the Constitution's drafters were almost all politicians, but, as my Grandma Ratter says, they sure don't make things like they used to.

Research and Analysis (Logistics)

The states must also plan for the logistics of the actual Convention, including date, time and location, as well as meals, transportation and housing for 250 delegates and staff.

Date and time can be coordinated in the state resolutions, like the First of June following the passage of the 34th state resolution. Technically speaking, under Article V, once 34 state resolutions are printed in the National Register, Congress is supposed to "Call" the Convention. So, what happens if Congress doesn't "call" something...whatever that means anyway? By agreeing on a time and place before hand, the states can make the process entirely automatic. As long as the States send the resolutions to the National Archivist, who publishes them in the Statutes at Large and National Register, it's perfectly legal.

As to location, if isolation is important, as it was for the First Convention, I recommend a remote state park with lodging where delegates could meet for weeks on end. Event organizers can handle meals, transportation, laundry, and any similar necessities. And, as for who pays the bills, each state would be responsible for its own delegates.

Debating and Adopting a Resolution

Only the legislative leadership can authorize debate and allow a vote, so We the People must keep up the pressure until 34 resolutions are passed! Keep the faith, and don't grow weary in doing good work!

Part Four: Convention Time!
Timeline: 2040-2045

Once we've elected the Article V supporters and persuaded the state legislatures to pass the resolutions naming delegates, identifying issues, and setting the date, time and location of the convention, we will still need to run America's Second Constitutional Convention. Thankfully, we've done this before, albeit in 1787, so we can follow the steps they took. Here is an explanation of the procedures used by the First Constitutional Convention, and some suggestions for the second time around. It could take two weeks, or the Delegates may have to work for a few months, but the more we prepare before the Convention, the easier their work will be.

At the Convention, voting will be by State, and each State gets one vote. The State's vote is determined by the majority of the State's delegates.[164] The First Constitutional Convention allowed each State to determine its own number of delegates (Delaware had 5 and New York had 3), but only one vote per State. So things don't get out of hand, I suggest there's a limit of 5 delegates per state, for a total of 250.

The Great Delegate Commissioning

It's not every day history is made, and I think each State should relish it, and send its delegates with pomp, circumstance, and a full commissioning ceremony to make it official. A ceremony will also be the ideal setting for delegates to make a public oath to abide by the limits of the legislative resolution. Technically, a breach of the promise would be subject to the penalties of perjury…but I doubt it would ever have to come to that.

Again, people should not worry that a Convention will be a "free-for-all," and that once called, delegates can change whatever they'd like. As in 1787, each state's delegates will be limited by the scope of authority in the state's resolution, and the courts could deem any unauthorized amendment illegal and unenforceable. And, just as in 1787, each delegate must provide a sealed document from the clerk of the state legislature before allowed in the Convention, which will also provide limits on how the delegate can vote. The ratification process will provide another enforcement mechanism to ensure delegates stay inbounds, because the states can refuse to ratify the proposed amendments that they didn't authorize in the first place.

Time is also on our side, when it comes to staying within the bounds of the state resolutions. We've waited 225 years for change, so what's the big deal if we need to wait a few more for the Third Convention? If an idea is genius today, it is genius forever…just like our Constitution and Article V.

Procedures

Most of the rules from the Convention of 1787 will work just fine today. They may seem harsh in the Information Age, but they are designed to maintain professionalism, to motivate hard work, and to deter would-be delegates who can't handle this sort of pressure.

First, the Convention should again operate in secret, because it's easier to negotiate a settlement behind closed doors, and easier to get work done in peace and quiet. When I work, I go to a library, not a media circus. I also think we should adopt the former rule that no records of votes are kept, other than if a vote passes. In 1787 there were no external publications of the proceedings; only Delegates could inspect the journal of proceedings (including after the Convention), and absolutely nothing spoken could be printed or published in any way without permission of the Delegates. I realize that in an age when the President feels the need to set up a twit account, it may be difficult to find people mature enough to keep a secret, but that's a good thing, because we don't want average delegates, do we?

Second, the work of the Convention should be done in specialized committees, its members elected by delegates, with one committee for each amendment topic, like term limits. Committee members are the experts to perform analysis and prepare reports, and the full Convention makes the final decisions. Ideally, delegates will propose an amendment by motion, or submit it to the clerk, and the President of the Convention will refer it to a committee for review and report. Committees will be responsible for analyzing all proposals, and submitting their best attempt at fixing the underlying problem with the Constitution.

Committees could (should) also draft commentaries on the meaning of an amendment's specific language, and what the Convention did not intend. One of the biggest problems with our current Constitution is that courts don't have much to guide their interpretation, apart from the unofficial journal kept by Madison and newspaper articles written after the fact. The Supreme Court tries its best to find guidance in the few words and phrases recorded during debates, but that's less than ideal. This time, let's plan ahead and prepare official commentaries to avoid confusion in the future and make enforcement easier.

If any logistical changes within the government are required, like changes in voting rules, the proposed amendments should provide the logistics and timeline for reasonable implementation, like staggering term limits or grandfathering in certain judges or representatives. The committees should also include an analysis of the expense associated with a particular amendment. In a day when people do as little as possible to help each other, the Convention will need to go the extra mile and map this out in the greatest detail possible. The stakes couldn't be any higher, and the Delegates' efforts should be commensurate with their task.

Third, the 1787 Convention required all delegates to respect each other and the significance of their work (as opposed to the political malarky seen on C-Span). They chose a President from the group to keep order and to follow the rules (George Washington). The President's decisions on procedure are final. Delegates stood for the President. When Delegates spoke, they addressed the President. When a Delegate spoke, no other Delegate could pass notes, talk with each other, or read anything...which in today's language means no electronic devices of any sort. (Choosing the right delegate is essential.) Any Delegate can be called out for acting the fool. Maintaining respect and order is necessary to ensure cooperation and to minimize strife.

Fourth, they followed basic procedures for running an orderly meeting, like reading all motions twice and dividing compound questions. Today, we use Robert's Rules of Order for things like this. Every morning, the Secretary (also elected by Delegates) read the minutes of the preceding day. Delegates could only speak twice on any question, and the second was only after everyone else had a chance to talk.

Of course, there were carefully calculated votes, debates over word choice, private meetings between State delegations, and such. That's to be expected, and will make the assembly quite interesting, but, like the Manhattan Project, the world may never know all the effort that will go into the final result.

Proposing Amendments

At the end of the Convention, the delegates will debate and either adopt or reject the amendments proposed by the committees. For those proposed amendments fortunate enough to be adopted by the entire Convention, they must make their way back to the National Archivist for the ratification process.

Part Five: Ratification
Timeline: 2045-2050

We already have the procedure in place for ratification.[165] After the Convention is over, the National Archivist will take the proposed amendments and create information packets to send to the 50 state governors, who will then forward to their legislatures for ratification. As I said previously, this will ensure that the delegates do not exceed their authority by completely re-writing the Constitution. The legislatures will then vote, and send certified copies of the ratification to the Archivist according to current precedent and law. The proposed amendments will become part of the Constitution once ratified by three-fourths (38 of 50) of the states.

The amendments themselves will make changes that could take time to implement, like modifying the number and size of Congressional districts and the way we run federal elections. Others, like term limits, won't really change much. The point is, as soon as the Amendments are ratified, there may still be work to do.

2051: **America's New & Improved Government**

2075: **Third Constitutional Convention (And every 25 years thereafter)**

2100: **Fourth Constitutional Convention**

Well…what are you waiting for? Let's get to it!

"I'd love my job, if it weren't for the paper cuts."

Robert D.W. Connor
First Archivist of the United States
(Archivist: 1934–1941)

PART THREE:

(LOW BUDGET)
FILL-IN-THE-BLANK DOCUMENTS

Draft State Resolution

S T A T E   O F   [INSERT]

RESOLUTION No. _____

201x-20xx Regular Sessions

I N   A S S E M B L Y

[DATE]

Introduced by Representative [NAME] read once and referred to the Committee on [NAME], committee discharged, Resolution amended, ordered reprinted as amended and recommitted to said committee

THE PEOPLE OF THE STATE OF [STATE], REPRESENTED IN [Lower Chamber] AND [Upper Chamber], DO RESOLVE AS FOLLOWS:

WE ACKNOWLEDGE our Duty as American Citizens to Use our Best Efforts to:
- form a more perfect Union;
- establish Justice;
- insure domestic Tranquility;
- provide for the common defence;
- promote the general Welfare; and
- secure the Blessings of Liberty to ourselves and our Posterity;

WE ACKNOWLEDGE, in the words of George Washington, that the basis of our political system is the right of the people to make and to alter their constitutions of government; and

WE ACKNOWLEDGE, in the words of Abraham Lincoln, that Whenever the American People shall grow weary of the existing government, they can exercise their constitutional right of amending it.

THEREFORE,

§ 1: REQUEST FOR LIMITED CONVENTION TO PROPOSE CERTAIN AMENDMENTS

We Hereby Make a Formal Request to the Congress that a LIMITED Constitutional Convention, to be Composed of five (5) Delegates from each State, one of whom must be the State's Chief Judge, or, the Chief Judge's Personal Agent, ORGANIZED as further addressed below be Called by the Congress for Proposing Amendments to solve the FOLLOWING PROBLEMS with the current CONSTITUTION of 1787:

[AMENDMENTS TO BE IDENTIFIED BY SUBJECT]

1. Imposing TERM LIMITS on the Members of the House of Representatives;
2. Requiring a BALANCED BUDGET be PASSED by the CONGRESS by DATE each year, and to prohibit the FORMAL and PARTY LEADERSHIP of the CONGRESS from RE-ELECTION as a PENALTY for Failure to Comply;
3. Requiring ANNUAL EXPENDITURE to PAY OFF the NATION'S DEBT in an amount of ONE and ONE-HALF TIMES the INTEREST PAYMENTS on ALL

DEBT, but NOT more than SEVEN and ONE-HALF PERCENT of the NATIONAL BUDGET;

4. FILL IN THE BLANKS...

FURTHER, This Convention shall be called within 6 months of the passage of a similar Resolution by the NUMBER THIRTY-FOURTH Sister State, as CONFIRMED by the NATIONAL ARCHIVIST in the same FORM and MANNER as for RATIFICATION, and State shall appropriate funds for in amount similar to current per-diem for basic government employees.

FURTHER, OUR FORMAL REQUEST is LIMITED to the EXPRESS TOPICS Described herein, and we DO NOT REQUEST or AUTHORIZE the CONVENTION to Propose Amendments on topics BEYOND those DESCRIBED HEREIN.

§ 2: PROHIBITION AGAINST MODIFICATION OF CERTAIN RIGHTS

OUR FORMAL REQUEST expressly PROHIBITS the CONVENTION from Altering any of the following portions of the BILL of RIGHTS and SUBSEQUENT AMENDMENTS:

- THE FIRST AMENDMENT, with the EXCEPTION of separate treatment of CAMPAIGN SPEECH;
- THE SECOND AMENDMENT
- THE THIRD AMENDMENT
- THE FOURTH AMENDMENT
- ETC.

§ 3: PROCEDURES FOR THE CONSTITUTIONAL CONVENTION

The CONVENTION'S PROCEEDINGS shall be Closed to the PUBLIC and KEPT SECRET by the DELEGATES and INVITEES.

Each State may call, in addition to five (5) Delegates, five (5) additional ADVISORS over the course of the Convention.

The CONVENTION shall abide by the RULES of the CONSTITUTIONAL CONVENTION held from MONDAY, MAY 25 to SEPTEMBER 17, 1787, including, but not limited to, the following[166]:

- The RULES shall not allow for the CALLING of Roll on Votes for the yeas & nays and have them entered on the minutes;
- Immediately after the President shall have taken the chair, and the members their seats, the minutes of the preceding day shall be read aloud by the Secretary;
- Every member, rising to speak, shall address the President; and whilst (s)he shall be speaking, none shall pass between them, or hold discourse with another, or read a book, pamphlet or paper, printed or manuscript [OR USE ANY FORM OF ELECTRONIC DEVICE THAT IS CONNECTED TO THE INTERNET];
- A member shall not speak more often than twice, without special leave, upon the same question; and not the second time, before every other, who had been silent, shall have been heard, if (s)he choose to speak upon the subject;
- A motion made and seconded, shall be repeated, and if written, as it shall be when any member shall so require, read aloud by the Secretary, before it shall be debated; and may be withdrawn at any time, before the vote upon it shall have been declared;

- Orders of the day shall be read next after the minutes, and either discussed or postponed, before any other business shall be introduced;
- When a debate shall arise upon a question, no motion, other than to amend the question, to commit it, or to postpone the debate shall be received;
- A question which is complicated, shall, at the request of any member, be divided, and put separately on the propositions, of which it is compounded;
- The determination of a question, altho' fully debated, shall be postponed, if the delegates of any State desire it until the next day;
- A writing which contains any matter brought on to be considered, shall be read once throughout for information, then by paragraphs to be debated, and again, with the amendments, if any, made on the second reading; and afterwards, the question shall be put on the whole, amended, or approved in its original form, as the case shall be;
- Committees shall be appointed by ballot; and the members who have the greatest number of ballots, altho' not a majority of the votes present, shall be the Committee;
- When two or more members have an equal number of votes, the member standing first on the list in the order of taking down the ballots, shall be preferred;
- A member may be called to order by any other member, as well as by the President; and may be allowed to explain his/her conduct or expressions deemed reprehensible;
- All questions of order shall be decided by the President without appeal or debate;
- Upon a question to adjourn for the day, which may be made at any time, if it be seconded, the question shall be put without a debate;
- When the House shall adjourn, every member shall stand in his place, until the President pass him/her;

- There shall be no Interruption of business by absence of members, or licentious publications of their proceedings;
- The CONVENTION is not to be precluded by a vote upon any question, from revising the subject matter of it when they see cause, nor, on the other hand, be led too hastily to rescind a decision, which was the result of mature discussion;
- That no member be absent from the House, so as to interrupt the representation of the State, without leave;
- That Committees do not sit whilst the House shall be or ought to be, sitting;
- That no copy be taken of any entry on the journal during the sitting of the House without leave of the House;
- That members only be permitted to inspect the journal; and
- That nothing spoken in the House be printed, or otherwise published or communicated without leave.

§ 4: LOGISTICS and COSTS

The CONVENTION shall be Called at [PLACE] on the First of May of the Year Immediately Following the Filing of the Thirty-Fourth State's Resolution calling for Convention with the National Archivist.

The STATE of [NAME] shall reserve funds for the DELEGATES to Attend the Convention, including reasonable travel, room and board, to be determined according to the system used for STATE employees.

The STATE shall also provide to each DELEGATE and ASSISTANT a per-diem compensation in the amount of [insert amount, like $100.00].

The Funds shall come from the budget of the Secretary of State of [NAME].

§ 5: DELEGATES

The STATE of [NAME] shall send the Following DELEGATES to the CONVENTION with LIMITED AUTHORITY to debate and to propose the CERTAIN AMENDMENTS identified above:

> DELEGATE CHIEF JUDGE, or PROXY
> DELEGATE TWO
> DELEGATE THREE
> DELEGATE FOUR
> DELEGATE FIVE

Each DELEGATE shall be allowed one Assistant to accompany the DELEGATE, to be paid for by the People of the STATE of [NAME].

In the event one or more DELEGATES becomes unable to continue to Represent the STATE OF [NAME], the following Alternate Delegates shall be sent to the Convention as a Replacement in this order:

> ALTERNATE DELEGATE ONE
> ALTERNATE DELEGATE TWO

§ 5: RATIFICATION

ANY Proposed AMENDMENTS must be RATIFIED by the Legislatures of 38 States to become a VALID PART of the CONSTITUTION, pursuant to the PROCEDURES of the NATIONAL ARCHIVIST;

THE PEOPLE of this STATE, through its LEGISLATURE, hereby AGREE to RATIFY the PROPOSED

AMENDMENTS by MAJORITY unless Seventy-Five Percent of this LEGISLATURE Votes Against Ratification.

§ 6: IMPLEMENTATION

A Certified Copy of this RESOLUTION shall be Delivered to the Archivist of the United States of America, who will then Publish it in accord with the procedures for the Publication of Ratification of Amendments to the Constitution. The Archivist shall also handle the Ratification of any Proposed Amendments

The CONGRESS is called on to act in accord herewith; however, even if CONGRESS does not issue a proclamation Calling for a Convention, We the PEOPLE of the STATE of [NAME] will send our Delegates to [PLACE] for the purpose of joining with Delegates from the Other States to propose Amendments.

Draft Introducer's Memorandum

To: The Members of the [HOUSE] of the State
            of [STATE]

From: Legislator [NAME]

Re: Resolution for Constitutional Convention

This Memorandum addresses the foregoing Resolution.

1. Purpose of the Resolution

The Purpose of this Resolution is to call together a Limited Convention of the Fifty United States of America to propose specific Amendments to the United States Constitution.

2. Summary of Provisions

This Resolution does the following.

First, it calls for a Convention to propose specific Amendments, including:

[SUMMARIZE FROM RESOLUTION]

Second, it identifies the following portions of the Constitution that shall not be Amended:

[SUMMARIZE FROM RESOLUTION]

Third, it articulates Procedural Rules for the Convention.

Fourth, it provides Logistics for sending Delegates.

Fifth, it identifies the proposed Delegates of the State of [NAME].

Sixth, it provides procedures for Ratification of Proposed Amendments.

Seventh, it provides for the Implementation of this Resolution.

3. Fiscal Impact on the State

The State will be required to pay for the Travel, Room and Board for Five (5) Delegates, plus one Assistant for each Delegate, for an indefinite period during the Convention, according to the current per diem expenses allowed for State employees.

Delegates shall also receive a STIPEND of (?).

The Funds shall come from the Budget of the Secretary of State.

4. Impact on Regulation of Businesses and Individuals

None

5. Fines, Imprisonment, Forfeiture of Rights, Sanctions

None

Delegate's Oath

I, _____ (name), do solemnly swear, and pledge to the people of the great State of [STATE], that I accept the public trust placed in me as a delegate to the second constitutional convention, that I will not betray that trust or exceed the limited authority granted to me, and that I will do my best to defend and protect the integrity of our great State, of our Federal Republic, and of our Constitution.

Newspaper Editorial

[Date]

Dear Editor:

There are plenty of things we want changed about Washington, DC. We want Representatives to work more, and to campaign less. We want Congress to get things done, instead of war-style politics where the winner takes all. We want campaigns that are not influenced by non-citizens without the right to vote—like corporations. The list goes on...

These problems are not caused by our current public servants. These problems are caused by the parts of the Constitution that are vague, outdated, have no enforcement mechanisms, and are silent on significant issues.

Until now, the only way we've Amended the Constitution is through Congress. But, if we're trying to use Amendments to clean up Washington, DC, we probably can't expect Congress to do it all by itself.

But Wait! There is a second way to amend the framework of our federal government that's never been tried before! Article V of the Constitution allows state legislatures to circumvent Washington, DC, and call their own convention to propose amendments. There has never been a state-called convention, and it's about time we call one.

What will it take to accomplish this? We need to elect representatives for our state legislature who are willing to change the nation, and to call for a limited convention to address the specific problems we're facing. It might take decades for us to pull it off, and to change the way we think about our government, but it will be worth it!

We've been taught that our Constitution is some concrete document with irrefutable truths that was sent down from on high. Well, that's true when we talk about the rights it protects, but, when it comes to government structure and powers, the Constitution is more like a family's secret recipe for brownies. It has specific ingredients in certain proportions, and those elements have been slowly refined over the years to get it to the delicious dish it is today.

Unfortunately, we've never adjusted our ingredients. After 225 years with our Constitution (ratified in 1788; new government installed 1790), I think we can see what parts of our government are leaving us sick...and it's time to change them.

Is it really that easy to change America? Can we really re-form our entire government without bloodshed, and just by voting for State elections over the next couple decades? Yes, it really is. So, let's join the effort, and vote for candidates that will call for convention.

- A Fellow American

Event Flyer

HEY _____!
<small>(CITY/GROUP)</small>

ARE YOU SICK AND TIRED OF POLITICIANS?

IS WASHINGTON DC GETTING YOU DOWN?

DO YOU FEEL LIKE NOTHING CAN CHANGE?

WELL!! GUESS WHAT!!

THINGS <u>CAN CHANGE</u>
WITH
YOUR VOTE IN STATE ELECTIONS!

"LET'S FIX THE PARTS OF THE
CONSTITUTION THAT ARE BROKEN!"

"LET'S PUT LIMITS ON GOVERNMENT!"

"LET'S CALL A CONSTITUTIONAL CONVENTION!!"

<u>COME HEAR MORE ABOUT SAVING AMERICA!</u>

_____
(EVENT)

_____
(DATE/TIME)

_____
(WHERE)

_____
(RSVP)

Write-In Candidate Campaign Postcards

_____ (*Name*)
IS HANDS DOWN MOST QUALIFIED
FOR

_____(*Office*)

NOT A REPUBLICAN
NOT A DEMOCRAT
JUST AN AMERICAN!

On Election Day, vote MOST QUALIFIED by
WRITING IN your choice. Bring this postcard to the
Ballot Box, and say you want to WRITE IN:

_____ (*Name*)

VOTE FOR:_____
FOR:_____
QUALIFICATIONS:

Liberty
FOREVER

[*FILL IN QUALIFICATIONS*]

WRITE IN YOUR CHOICE!!
NO MORE PARTY POLITICS!!
LET'S DO BETTER, AMERICA!!!

TO:

Letter (or Email) to State Representative

Your Name
Your Address
City, State and Zip Code

Date

Representative NAME
State Capitol
Capitol City, State, Zip Code

      Re: Article V Constitutional Convention

Dear Representative NAME:

**I live in your district, and am writing to ask
for YOUR help in cleaning up our federal government!**

For years, people across our State have complained about our federal leaders, and the [insert problems, like growing debt, partisan politics, corporate influence, unfair tax code, unfair voting system]. Well, it turns out that YOU have the power to rein in the President, the Congress and the Supreme Court, and I'm writing to ask that you please use it NOW! It's legal, it's peaceful, and it's the ONLY tool we have to stop the abuses of power in Washington DC.

During the Constitutional Convention of 1787, when George Washington, James Madison, John Hancock and others were busy designing the Congress, the Presidency and Supreme Court, they included a "check-and-balance" giving the States the upper hand over Washington DC...but in 225 years, the States have never once used it! Under Article V of the Constitution, if our State Legislature, along with 33 others, will pass resolutions calling for a *Second* Convention, then all 50 States can send Delegates to convene like they did 225 years ago, make changes to the blueprint for the federal government, and place real limits and consequences on our federal representatives.

America is made of 50 United States, and these same States that created our federal government have the ongoing responsibility to keep it streamlined, efficient, and responsive to We the People! After 225 years, there has been NO tune-up for our system, and we need YOUR help to make this happen. This will have nothing to do with our State's legislature, or how you do things in [CITY]. Our State is sovereign, and we are looking only to clean up the federal government.

Representative NAME
Date
Page 2

So...here's what you can do. Please help!

First, I include a draft Resolution for your consideration. We need representatives like you to propose resolutions across all States, and start the debate over an Article V Convention. As you can see, we're only looking for LIMITED changes to Washington DC, so the Convention will only address the issues you allow in the Resolution. Please, submit this proposed Resolution to the Clerk, and get co-sponsors!!

Second, we need the leaders in the [STATE BODY] to take action on this Resolution, submit it to Committee for review and hearings, and then to the Floor for debate and a vote. I and thousands of my fellow [State-ers] will be calling on you and other representatives to take ACTION!

Third, we need Americans like you to put aside party politics and stop worrying about re-election, and to DO what is best for the United States. Too long have our elected officials placed their careers over We the People. It is time for all of us to forget about ourselves, and to work toward this common goal.

Thousands of voters in your district want this Change, and we're going to get it one way or the other. It's our hope that you will help us, and that you will fulfill your responsibility to keep Washington DC in check. If not, we will find your replacement.

Thank you for your attention to this matter, and I look forward to working with you to help form a More Perfect Union!

Respectfully,

Name

Elevator Speech (also, see back cover)

Good news My Fellow Americans!

Are you tired of our run-down, overly-political federal government? Are you sick of watching politicians put their interests first, at the expense of We the People? Are you fed up with the same cycle of broken campaign promises?

The answer to all our problems is the Article V Convention!

Yes, the Article V Convention lets We the People re-write the rulebook for Congress, the President and Supreme Court.

It's easy! All you do is vote for State representatives willing to put the federal government in its place! Mmmm…It's so tasty too! Tastes just like Liberty and Justice for All!

Article V is the only peaceful and legal tool We the People have to fix our run-down, broken heap of a government! Overspending, spiraling debt, corporate contributions, IRS abuses, and constant campaigning are only a few of the problems plaguing Washington DC that we can fix!

The America 2051 Project is a nationwide effort to persuade our state representatives to call a Convention! So, call your local representative, and tell them to support a Convention!

Let's Vote our way to Health!

Candidate Questionnaire

Name: _____   Date: _____

Office: _____   District: _____

Instructions: Please answer the following questions using complete sentences. Explain your answers. If more space is needed, attach additional pages as necessary. Please cite to all sources.

1.) Do you support an Article V convention? Why?

2.) What problems should the Convention address?

3.) What are your suggested solutions to these problems?

4.) Will you participate in a debate or panel discussion?

5.) Define "democracy".

6.) Whom would you nominate as delegates? Why?

7.) What leadership role(s) do you have in the legislature? How will you use your leadership role(s) to support a Convention?

8.) List your professional contacts who are willing to volunteer to analyze the problems identified above, and propose solutions.

THE
AMERICA 2051
PARTY KIT

Nicole's "Preparations" Checklist for a Great Party

Purpose of the Event
- Spend time thinking about the ultimate goal of the event; it may be to raise funds, raise awareness, celebrate an accomplishment, celebrate a milestone, thank someone etc...
- Document the goal

Guest List
- Identify the necessary people to have at the event to accomplish the goal

Save the Date (Samples On-Line)
- I don't care what type of event it is... I always love to send a Save the Date. This creates a buzz for the event. It also has people calling/ texting and asking if they received this.
- This should be a printed item — it can easily get lost via email in junk
- Save the dates shouldn't tell too much about the event – Just a clue into what is to come

Invitation (Samples On-Line)
- Depending on the guest list, invitations should go out 4-6 weeks in advance. Further out for more affluent individuals that may have a busy social and business calendar
- Make this invitation FUN & EXCITING and explains the goal of the event. It should affirm to guests that they cannot miss this event

Social Media in conjunction with invitation
- Have a Facebook page or website etc... that folks can log onto, post and create excitement about the event
- The host can post daily about preparation or sneak peaks into event to come

THE
AMERICA 2051
PARTY KIT

Nicole's "Day Of" Checklist for a Great Party

Décor
- Décor should always support the goal
- Consider the guests path of entry to venue — use fun signage & props to create an exciting entrance
- Don't forget music for atmosphere

Welcome
- Welcome guests immediately with friendly smile, "Thank You" for joining & provide a name tag so guests can easily interact with one another
- Hand guest a custom cocktail to get the party started!
- Do not hand any other materials at this time — guests need a free hand

Food:
- Array of Appetizers
- Choice of American Meal Options (See Brian's All-American Menus)
- Desserts

Bar
- Always provide an array of alcoholic and non-alcoholic options
- Make sure your non-alcoholic options are just as exciting as the rest
- Add into the bar area fun props that support your goal
- Provide themed straws, garnish, stemware & beverage napkins
- Create themed framed signage to show guests bar selections

Activities (Instructions On-Line)
- Party Games (Pin the Peg-Leg on Mr. Morris, available online!)
- All-American Trivia
- Sharing the Good News!

Parting Gift
- ALWAYS provide a parting gift — maybe for the America 2051 party, it's a simple cellophane bag of (2) chocolate chip cookies (So American) with a ribbon & tag to reinforce the goal

Follow Up
- Within 48hrs, I like to have someone make phone calls and thank guests for attending and for any donations they may have made.
- Within 5 business days, I like to send a hand written thank you note on stationary that is goal driven and signed by the host
- Keep updating social media showing the success of the event
- Post the next party date for guests to mark their calendars!

170

THE
AMERICA 2051
PARTY KIT

Brian's All-American Menus
(recipes online)

Self-Serve Appetizers
- Classic Deviled Eggs
- Sloppy Joe Sliders
- Mom's Meatloaf Bites
- Veggies and Fruits

Menu #1:   Simple and Classic
- All-American Hamburger & Hotdog Cookout
- Cheese, Lettuce, Tomato, Ketchup, Mustard, Relish on Soft Potato Buns
- Mom's No-Mayo Mac Salad
- Mom's Sour Cream Cucumber Salad
- Calico Baked Beans
- Corn on the Cob
- Warm Apple Pie

Menu #2:   Kick it up a notch
- BBQ Smoked Baby Back Ribs & Southern Country Fried Chicken
- Aunt Bev's Kansas Coleslaw
- Creamy Bacon Potato Salad
- Mom's Tomato Salad
- Corn Bread
- Blueberry Cobbler w/ Vanilla Bean Ice Cream

Bar
- Always provide an array of alcoholic and non-alcoholic options
- Drink domestic!
- Make sure your non-alcoholic options are just as exciting as the rest
- Add into the bar area fun props that support your goal
- Provide themed straws, garnish, stemware & beverage napkins
- Create themed framed signage to show guests bar selections

Party Invitations

YOU'RE CORDIALLY INVITED TO

_____'S

FOR AN ARTICLE V CONVENTION PARTY!

THERE IS A WAY TO FIX WASHINGTON DC!
ALL IT WILL TAKE IS YOUR VOTE IN STATE ELECTIONS!
LET'S CELEBRATE AND LEARN MORE!

ON _____ AT _____ O'CLOCK AM / PM
AT _____

RSVP TO:_____

FOR MORE INFO:

AMERICA2051.COM

Bookmarks / Parting Gifts
(Print On Thick Paper)

ARTICLE V OF THE UNITED STATES CONSTITUTION

The Congress, whenever two thirds of both houses shall deem it necessary, shall propose amendments to this Constitution, or, <u>on the application of the legislatures of two thirds of the several states, shall call a convention for proposing amendments</u>, which, in either case, shall be valid to all intents and purposes, as part of this Constitution, when ratified by the legislatures of three fourths of the several states, or by conventions in three fourths thereof, as the one or the other mode of ratification may be proposed by the Congress; provided that no amendment which may be made prior to the year one thousand eight hundred and eight shall in any manner affect the first and fourth clauses in the ninth section of the first article; and that no state, without its consent, shall be deprived of its equal suffrage in the Senate.

ARTICLE V OF THE UNITED STATES CONSTITUTION

The Congress, whenever two thirds of both houses shall deem it necessary, shall propose amendments to this Constitution, or, <u>on the application of the legislatures of two thirds of the several states, shall call a convention for proposing amendments</u>, which, in either case, shall be valid to all intents and purposes, as part of this Constitution, when ratified by the legislatures of three fourths of the several states, or by conventions in three fourths thereof, as the one or the other mode of ratification may be proposed by the Congress; provided that no amendment which may be made prior to the year one thousand eight hundred and eight shall in any manner affect the first and fourth clauses in the ninth section of the first article; and that no state, without its consent, shall be deprived of its equal suffrage in the Senate.

GOOD NEWS, AMERICA!

WE THE PEOPLE CAN FIX WASHINGTON DC!

IN 1787, THEY PUT ONE CHECK-AND-BALANCE IN THE
CONSTITUTION TO CURB EXCESS POWER IN OUR FEDERAL GOVERNMENT,
BUT WE HAVE NEVER ONCE TRIED IT!

UNDER ARTICLE V, THE FIFTY STATES CAN CALL A
SECOND CONSTITUTIONAL CONVENTION TO UPDATE
THE 225-YEAR-OLD RULES FOR HOW CONGRESS,
THE PRESIDENT AND THE SUPREME COURT OPERATE!

WHAT WE CAN CHANGE   OUR LOCAL REPRESENTATIVES

1.
2.
                  SUPPORTS: _____ YES _____ NO
3.
4.
                  SUPPORTS: _____ YES _____ NO
5.
6.
                  SUPPORTS: _____ YES _____ NO
7.
8.

MORE INFO AT:

AMERICA2051.COM

Use your imagination…

Notes

**Copies of all on-line sources
are available at America2051.com.**

[1] United States Constitution, National Archives (online).

[2] "Washington's Farewell Address 1796," Yale Law School, Avalon Project (online). Painting: "The Athenaeum," Gilbert Stuart,1796 (Wikipedia Commons).

[3] New York State's motto is *excelsior*. University of Rochester's is *meliora*.

[4] The same day I handed my neighbor a draft of this essay, he gave me a copy of Mark Levin's book, *The Liberty Amendments*. The similarities between these two works are understandable as we are both lawyers, but I can proudly say that I took a more practical, non-political, and light-hearted approach. I can only hope that this Project is the sort of effort Mr. Levin and others will support as an actual roadmap to Convention.

[5] "Teddy Roosevelt Would Never Get Elected in 2014," John Dickerson, Sept 12, 2014, Slate.com.

[6] "Here Is Every Previous Government Shutdown, Why they Happened, and How They Ended," Dylan Matthews, The Washington Post (online), Sept 25, 2013.

[7] www.usdebtclock.org

[8] I recognize this is an extremely generic statement, and that there were (and are) conflicting views among rational Americans as to how best to distribute power among the people...but that's topic for another day.

[9] Madison, James, *Notes of Debates in the Federal Convention of 1787*, Ohio University Press, 1966, pg 649. *See also* "Soldier-Statesmen of the Constitution," Robert K. Wright, Jr. and Morris J. MacGregor, Jr., Center of Military History, United States Army, Washington, D.C., 1987; "Gouverneur Morris" US Army (online) accessed Nov 14, 2015; "Gouverneur Morris," The Netherland Institute (online) accessed April 5, 2015; Image: Wikipedia Commons.

[10] "Gouverneur Morris," Teaching American History (online), accessed Nov 19, 2015; "Soldier-Statesmen of the Constitution," Robert K. Wright, Jr. and Morris J. MacGregor, Jr., Center of Military History, United States Army, Washington, D.C., 1987; "Creating a Constitution," Library of Congress (online), accessed Dec 30, 2015; "The Man Who Wrote the Words 'We the People'," National Constitution Center (online), accessed Dec 30, 2015; Brookhiser, Richard, "The Forgotten Founding Father," City Journal, Spring 2002.

[11] "Soldier-Statesmen of the Constitution," Robert K. Wright, Jr. and Morris J. MacGregor, Jr., Center of Military History, United States Army, Washington, D.C., 1987; *see also* "America's Founding Fathers, Gouverneur Morris," National Archives (online), accessed Nov 15, 2015; W. David Samuelsen, "Manor of Morrisania and the Early Morrises," USGenWebArchives (online), accessed Dec 30, 2015; "Gouverneur Morris," Wikipedia (online) accessed Nov 15, 2015.

[12] "Delegates to the Constitutional Convention/Gouverneur Morris", Teaching American History (online), accessed Nov 15, 2015.

[13] See note 10.

[14] See note 9.

[15] "Scene of Gouverneur Morris's Accident", Teaching American History (online), accessed Nov 19, 2015; "Gouverneur Morris 1757-1816," Gouverneur, NY Museum (online), accessed Dec 30, 2015.

[16] Roosevelt, Theodore, *American Statesmen, Gouverneur Morris*, Houghton, Mifflin and Company, Cambridge 1892.

[17] Id.

[18] "Gouverneur Morris" History.com Staff (online) 2009.

[19] Madison, James, *Notes of Debates in the Federal Convention of 1787*, Ohio University Press, 1966, pg 649.

[20] Id.

[21] Id. at 24: "On reading the credentials of the deputies it was noted that those from Delaware were prohibited from changing the article in the confederation establishing an equality of votes among the States."

[22] "Congress Sets Record for Voting Along Party Lines", Elaine Izadi, National Journal (online), Feb 3, 2014.

[23] "Forty percent of weekdays, Congress isn't in session," Philip Bump, The Washington Post (online), July 9, 2014. And, that does not include summers and holidays off...

[24] "Hope and Change: National Debt Tops $18 Trillion," Jason Peirce, Voices of Liberty (online), Mar 16, 2015.

[25] "President Obama will propose tax breaks for families financed with higher taxes on wealthy" Bruce Alpert, Time-Picayune, Jan 18, 2015.

[26] "2012 Presidential Election Cost Hits $2 Billion Mark," Stephen Braun and Jack Gillum, Associated Press & Huffington Post, Dec 6, 2012, updated Feb 5, 2013; "Cost to win congressional election skyrockets," Paul Steinhauser and robert Yoon, CNN.com, July 11, 2013.

[27] "Donor Demographics," Center for Responsive Politics (online) accessed Nov 14, 2015.

[28] "Small Pool of Rich Donors Dominates Election Giving," Nicholas Confessore, Sarah Cohen and Karen Yourish, New York Times (online), Aug 1, 2015.

[29] "Citygroup, Inc. Summary," Center for Responsive Politics (online) accessed Nov 14, 2015.

[30] "Honeywell Takes the Lead in Political Giving," Andy Pastor and Brody Mullins, The Wall Street Journal Online, Oct 13, 2010.

[31] "Commercial Banks" Center for Responsive Politics (online) accessed Nov 14, 2015.

[32] "Billionaires Tom Steyer, Michael Bloomberg Are Top Disclosing Political Donors in America," Dan Alexander, Forbes (online) Aug 7, 2014; see also "Top Individual Contributors - 2014," Center for Responsive Politics (online) accessed Nov 15, 2015 ("Here are the individuals who have dipped deepest into their own pockets for campaign contributions to federal candidates, parties, political action committees, 527 organizations, and Carey committees. Only contributions to Democrats and Republicans or liberal and conservative outside groups are included in calculating the percentages the donor has given to either party").

[33] "IRS Announces 2015 Tax Brackets, Standard Deduction Amounts And More," Kelly Phillips Erb, Forbes Online, Oct. 30, 2014.

[34] "Budget Deficit Returns to Pre-recession Levels" Jonathan House, The Wall Street Journal Online, Oct 15, 2015.

[35] "IRS Announces 2014 Tax Brackets, Standard Deduction Amounts And More", Kelly Phillips Erb, Oct 31, 2013, Forbes Online.

[36] "Budget in Brief", US Department of the Treasury, IRS.gov; "FBI opens criminal probe of tax agency, audit cites disarray" David Ingram and Matt Spetalnick, May 15, 2013, Reuters.

[37] "Semi-Presidential System" Wikipedia, accessed Nov 16, 2015.

[38] "Record-High 42% of Americans Identify as Independents", Jeffrey M. Jones, Jan 8, 2014, Gallup Online.

[39] "Congress Sets Record for Voting Along Party Lines", Elaine Izadi, Feb 3, 2014, National Journal Online.

[40] "Federal shutdown closes Statute of Liberty and other top tourist sites" Holly Bailey, Oct 1, 2013, Yahoo News.

[41] "Here is every previous government shutdown, why they happened and how they ended" Dylan Matthews, The Washington Post (online), Sept 25, 2013.

[42] "The Tortuous, Protracted Wait to Confirm Judges—From Abe to Obama" Russell Wheeler, The Atlantic, Feb 25, 2015.

[43] Jon Meacham, *Thomas Jefferson: The Art of Power*, Random House, 2013, pg 213.

[44] "The Constitutional Amendment Process," National Archives Website, accessed Nov 19, 2015.

[45] "Finding Aid to the Agassiz Garden Club Records," Institute for Regional Studies & University Archives, North Dakota State University Libraries, accessed Nov 19, 2015.
"Tennessee Eastman Recreation - Bowling Club Constitution and By-Laws" accessed Nov 19, 2015.

[46] "Democracy Index" Wikipedia, accessed Nov 19, 2015.

[47] Jon Meacham, Thomas Jefferson: The Art of Power, Random House, 2013, pg 320.

[48] "Statue of Liberty Reopens as Other Sites Stay Closed - The New York Times" Thomas Kaplan, Oct 13, 2013.

[49] "A Bankrupt Greece Is Struggling to Stay Afloat - The New York Times" Liz Alderman and Jack Weing, July 1, 2015.

[50] "Budget Deficit Returns to Pre-recession Levels" Jonathan House, The Wall Street Journal Online, Oct 15, 2015.

[51] "Fiscal Year 2016 Historical Tables, Budget of the U.S. Government," The White House (online) accessed Nov 19, 2015, Table 1.1.

[52] "Policy Basics/ Where Do Our Federal Tax Dollars Go?" Center on Budget and Policy Priorities, March 11, 2015, accessed Nov 19, 2015.

[53] "Japan Now Holds More U.S. Debt than China", Charles Riley, CNN Money, April 15, 2015.

[54] "National Debt Interest Payments Dwarf Other Government Spending" Danielle Kurtzleben, US News and World Report Online, Nov 19, 2012. See also Note 49.

[55] "$37 screws, a $7,622 coffee maker, $640 toilet seats; : suppliers to our military just won't be oversold" Jack Smith, Los Angeles Times, July 30, 1986.

[56] "$1.6B of Bank Bailout Went to Execs," Frank Bass and Rita Beamish, The Associated Press, Dec 21, 2008; "The Size of the Bank Bailout: $29 Trillion", John Carney, CNBC, Dec 11, 2011.

[57] "GM Bonuses Paid To White-collar, Blue-collar Workers Top $500 Million", Tom Krisher, The Associated Press, Feb 29, 2012.

[58] "Senate Approves Suspension of US Debt Ceiling," Janet Hook, The Wall Street Journal (online), Feb 12, 2014.

[59] "Seniority in the United States House of Representatives," Wikipedia, accessed April 5, 2015. The math comes out as follows: 0 - 8 Years = 37%; 8 + Years = 63%; 10+ = 169/435 = 0.38850575; 20+ = 82/435 = 0.18850575.

[60] "'Slaughter Solution' not bulletproof," Fred Barbash, Politico, Mar 16, 2010.

[61] "Term of Office" Wikipedia, accessed Nov 19, 2015.

[62] Id.

[63] "Forty percent of weekdays, Congress isn't in session," Philip Bump, The Washington Post (online) July 9, 2014. (This doesn't include summers off, or other recesses.)

[64] Sample Daily Schedule, Congressman Larry Buschon, M.D., IN-8 at http://bucshon.house.gov/sample-daily-schedule, accessed Sept 20. 2014.

[65] "Open Source with Steve Wozniak," (Interactive Transcript) OnInnovation, accessed Nov 19, 2015.

[66] Id.

[67] "Secret Service Prostitution Scandal/ One Year Later," Shane Harris, Washingtonian Online, March 25, 2013.

[68] "Hanging Chads; As the Florida Recount Implodes, the Supreme Court Decides Bush v. Gore," Samantha Levine, US News and World Report Online, Jan 17, 2008.

[69] Richard L. Smith, A Statistical Assessment of Buchanan's Vote in Palm Beach County, Statist. Sci. Vo. 17, Issue 4 (2002), 441-457; see also "Pat Admits: They're Not My Votes -- or Gores," Marilyn Rauber, New York Post (online), Nov 10, 2000.

[70] "2000 Presidential General Election Results," Federal Election Commission, accessed April 15, 2015.

[71] Bush v. Gore, 531 U.S. 98 (2000).

[72] "Counting the Lost Votes of Election 2000", Jessica Reaves, Time Magazine Online, Jul 17, 2001.

[73] "How The U.S. And Canadian Election Processes Differ" City News, News Staff, Nov 3, 2008.

[74] "USPS Loses $1.9 Billion in Second Quarter Despite Operating Profits", Eric Katz, Government Executive (online), May 9, 2015.

[75] "Ways to Vote", Elections Canada (online), accessed April 15, 2015.

[76] "US Electoral College: Frequently Asked Questions" US National Archives (online) accessed Nov 19, 2015.

[77] "Wyoming QuickFacts from the US Census Bureau", United States Census Bureau, accessed Nov 19, 2015.

[78] "New York QuickFacts from the US Census Bureau", United States Census Bureau, accessed Nov 19, 2015.

[79]Image from: http://philippineslifestyle.com/blog/2014/12/13/jesus-quevenco-unique-friendship-ferdinand-marcos/

[80] "Quick Answers to General Questions: Can non-US Citizens Contribute?" Federal Election Commission (online), accessed Nov 19, 2015.

[81] Ed Rollins with Tom DeFrank, *Bare Knuckles and Back Rooms: My Life in American Politics* (New York: Broadway, 1996), pp 214-215 in Russ Baker, *Family of Secrets: The Bush Dynasty, America's Invisible Government, and the Hidden History of the Last Fifty Years*, (Bloomsbury Press, 2009), pg. 349.

[82] "The Size of the Bank Bailout: $29 Trillion", John Carney, CNBC (online), Dec 14, 2011.

[83] "Donor Demographics," Center for Responsive Politics (online) accessed Nov 14, 2015.

[84] "Mad Money: TV Ads in the 2012 Presidential Campaign" and "2012 Presidential Campaign Finance Explorer", The Washington Post (online), accessed Nov 19, 2015.

[85] "How Much Money Goes to Breast Cancer Research?" Breast Cancer Consortium (online), accessed Nov 19, 2015.

[86] McCutcheon v. FEC, 134 S. Ct. 1434, 1449 (U.S. 2014).

[87] McCutcheon v. FEC, 134 S. Ct. 1434, 1441 (U.S. 2014).

[88] Valentine v. Chrestensen, 316 U.S. 52, 54 (1942).

[89] "Holocaust Denial -- Crime or Free Speech?", Tom Zeller, Jr., The New York Times (online), Feb 15, 2007.

[90] Schenck v. United States, 249 U.S. 47 (1919).

[91] Citizens United v. Federal Election Commission, No. 08-205, 558 U.S. 310 (2010)

[92] "Eastman Kodak employment continues to shrink," Mike Dickinson, Rochester Business Journal, March 20, 2014.

[93] "Kodak retirees lose health, welfare benefits", Matthew Daneman and Tom Tobin, USA Today, Nov. 6, 2012.

[94] "Proposed Retiree Benefit Changes Questions & Answers" Kodak.com, Nov. 2, 2012.

[95] "Kodak Bankruptcy Officially Ends", Matthew Daneman, USA Today, Sept 3, 2013.

[96] "Former Kodak CEO received $6.71M package in '13", Matthew Daneman, Democrat & Chronicle, April 15, 2014.

[97] "Detroit - The Ruins of an Empire/ A Conversation with Photographers Marchand and Meffre", Kisa Lala, Huffington Post, Jan 31, 2011.

[98] "President Obama Hosts 6 Fundraisers Friday in Minneapolis, Chicago Visit", Devin Dwyer, ABC News, June 1, 2012.

[99] "Honeywell, America's Top Political Donor, Has Received $13 Billion in Federal Money", Mike Elk, Huffington Post, May 25, 2011; see also "Honeywell Takes the Lead in Political Giving," Andy Pasztor and Brody Mullins, The Wall Street Journal Online, Oct 13, 2010.

[100] "Elizabeth Warren/ Citigroup Lobbyists 'Literally Wrote' Omnibus Bill" (Video) RealClearPolitics (online), accessed April 5, 2015; "$1.1tn US budget deal imperiled by revolt over taxpayer net for risky bank trades" Dan Roberts, The Guardian, Dec 11, 2014; "Elizabeth Warren was right/ The links between Citigroup and government run deep" Matt O'Brien and Darla Cameron, The Washington Post, Dec 16, 2014.

[101] "Citigroup Inc." Center for Responsive Politics (online) accessed Nov 14, 2015.

[102] Small pool of rich donors dominates election giving, Nicholas Confessore, Sarah Cohen and Karen Yourish, New York Times (online), Aug 1, 2015.

[103] "Supreme Court Strikes Down Overall Political Donation Cap," Adam Liptak, New York Times (online), Apr 2, 2014.

[104] "Citigroup Wrote the Wall Street Giveaway The House Just Approved," Erika Eichelberger, MotherJones.com Dec 10, 2014; "Citigroup Becomes the Fall Guy in the Spending Bill Battle," Michael Corkery, New York Times, Dec 12, 2014.

[105] "Liberals, Conservatives Gripe About $1.1 Trillion Bill," David Espo and Andrew Taylor, The Associated Press, Dec 10, 2014.

[106] "Contribution Limits Chart 2013-14", Federal Election Commission (online) accessed Nov 19, 2015.

[107] "Income and Poverty in the United States: 2013", Carmen DeNavas-Walt and Bernadette D. Proctor, U.S. Department of Commerce, September 2014.

[108] "Annual Update of the HHS Poverty Guidelines," Federal Register (online) Jan 24, 2013.

[109] "IRS: 235,413 million-dollar earners," Jennifer Epstein, Politico, Aug 5, 2011.

[110] "Top Individual Contributors: All Federal Contributions," Center for Responsive Politics (online) accessed Nov 15, 2015 ("Here are the individuals who have dipped deepest into their own pockets for campaign contributions to federal candidates, parties, political action committees, 527 organizations, and Carey committees. Only contributions to Democrats and Republicans or liberal and conservative outside groups are included in calculating the percentages the donor has given to either party").

[111] "Top Organization Contributions/ All Federal Contributions" Center for Responsive Politics (online) accessed April 15, 2015 ("Totals on this page reflect donations from employees of the organization, its PAC and in some cases its own treasury. These totals include all campaign contributions to federal candidates, parties, political action committees (including superPACs), federal 527 organizations, and Carey committees. Because 501(c) organizations do not disclose their donors, contributions to those groups are not included here, except in cases where the group discloses voluntarily. Only contributions to Democrats and Republicans or liberal and conservative outside groups are included in calculating the percentages the donor has given to either party").

[112] "Congress keeps free mail while pushing US postal cuts" Angela Greiling Keane, Bloomberg News, July 5, 2012.

[113] "The Money Behind the Elections" Center for Responsive Politics (online) accessed Nov 19, 2015.

[114]"House Reads Out Constitution, Only 74 Members Show Up," Steve Watson, FourWinds10.com, Jan 16, 2013.

[115] "Historical Highlights of the IRS", Irs.gov, accessed Nov 19, 2015.

[116] "IRS Announces 2015 Tax Brackets, Standard Deduction Amounts and More," Kelly Phillips Erb, Forbes Online, Oct. 30, 2014. See also "Income Tax in the United States," Wikipedia, accessed Nov 19, 2015.

[117] "Budget in Brief FY 2014," United States Treasury & Internal Revenue Service; "Tax Preparation Industry Analysis 2015 - Cost & Trends", FranchiseHelp.com, accessed Nov 16, 2015.

[118] "Warren Buffett urges 'shared sacrifice' as he defends tax plan to investors," Dominic Rushe, The Guardian, May 5, 2012.

[119] "Americans spend 6.1 billion hours on taxes," Charles Riley, CNN Money, Jan 5, 2011.

[120] "IRS officials in Washington were involved in targeting of conservative groups", Juliet Eilperin and Zachary A. Goldfarb, The Washington Post, May 13, 2013.

[121] "IRS Deliberately Cut Its Own Customer Service Budget" John McCormack, Weekly Standard, April 22, 2015.

[122] "2015 Poverty Guidelines", U.S. Department of Health and Human Services, accessed Nov 19, 2015.

[123] "Total Government Employment Since 1962", Office of Personnel Management, accessed Nov 19, 2015.

[124] "Being VP is just like being a lesser Kardashian," Dean Obeidallah, CNN.com Aug 3, 2012.

[125] "Searching for the first semi-presidential country -- Chile", Robert Elgie, Semi-Presidentialism Blog, Dublin City University; See Maurice Duverger, European Journal of Political Research, Vol. 8, Issue 2, pigs 165-187, June 1980.

[126] "Semi-Presidential System" Wikipedia, accessed Nov 16, 2015.

[127] Cole Joseph Harvey, "The Double-Headed Eagle: Semi-Presidentialism and Democracy in France and Russia," University of Pittsburgh, University Honors College, July 14, 2008.

[128] Id.

[129] "The Presidency Costs Taxpayers A Lot, But That's Not Obama's Fault", Doug Mataconis, Outside the Beltway (online) Sept. 29, 2012.

[130] "National Taxpayers Union - Which First Lady Flies Highest? Michelle vs. Laura" Diana Oprinescu, National Taxpayers Union (online) July 9, 2013.

[131] "How Big Is Michelle Obama's staff's budget?" George Spelvin, Western Journalism Online, Mar 27, 2012

[132] "Fight Erupts Over First Lady's Travel Costs," Paul Bedard, US News and World Report online, Oct. 5, 2011.

[133] "President, first lady take his and hers flights to LA," Betsy Klein and Kevin Liptak, CNN, March 13, 2015.

[134] "Michelle Obama Spain Trip Cost Taxpayers $467,000/ Judicial Watch" Elise Foley, The Huffington Post, April 26, 2012.

[135] "Barack and Michelle Obama took separate taxpayer-funded flights to LAX" Kieran Corcoran, The Daily Mail, March 14, 2015.

[136] "Michelle to Remain in Hawaii, Costing Taxpayers Over $100K," Keith Koffler, White House Dossier, Dec 26, 2012.

[137] "Michelle Obama sips tea with Prince Harry," Geoff Earle, New York Post, June 17, 2015.

[138] "Taxpayers Foot $128,781 For Michelle Obama's Sightseeing Trip To Venice," Steve Watson, InfoWars.com, June 16, 2015.

[139] "Voting with Party: House Democratic Caucus", Center for Responsive Politics (online) accessed Nov 19, 2015.

[140] "Voting with Party: House Republican Caucus," Center for Responsive Politics (online), accessed April 15, 2015.

[141] "Blame James Madison for the government shutdown," Michael Barone, Washington Examiner, Oct 2, 2013.

[142] *See,* John F. Kenney, *Profiles in Courage,* (Harper & Brothers), 1955.

[143] "Record-High 42% of Americans Identify as Independents", Jeffrey M. Jones, Gallup.com, Jan 8, 2014.

[144] Image: "ElectoralCollege1860" by AndyHogan14 - Own work. Licensed under Public domain via Wikimedia Commons.

[145] "ElectoralCollege2012" by Gage - Own work. Licensed under Public domain via Wikimedia Commons.

[146] "History of Proportional Representation," Proportional Representation Foundation (online), accessed Nov 19, 2015.

[147] Professor Douglas J. Amy, Department of Politics, Mount Holyoke College (online), accessed April 15, 2015.

[148] "Rehnquist's Illness Raises Stakes in Election" The Washington Times, Oct 26, 2004.

[149] New York State Constitution, Article VI, Section 25; see also "New York Mandatory Judicial Retirement Age Amendment, Proposal 6 (2013)", Balletopia.com (accessed 11-11-15).

[150] Lawrence Wrightsman, "Oral Arguments Before the Supreme Court: An Empirical Approach," Oxford University Press, Mar 17, 2008 at 8.

[151] "2004 term opinions of the Supreme Court of the United States" Wikipedia, accessed 11-19-15.

[152] "Rehnquist absent as court resumes work" The Associated Press, NBC News (online) Nov 1, 2004.

[153] "The Tortuous, Protracted Wait to Confirm Judges—From Abe to Obama" Russell Wheeler, The Atlantic, Feb 25, 2015.

[154] "Judicial Nominations and Confirmations: Fact and Fiction," Russell Wheeler, The Brookings Institution (online) Dec 30, 2013.

[155] "Bush Chooses Roberts for Court", Peter Baker and Jim VandeHei, The Washington Post (online), July 20, 2015.

[156] "Father of the Constitution", Montpelier Foundation (online), accessed 11-13-15.

[157] "Marley worked 'Night Shift' in Delaware", Robin Brown, The News Journal, July 22, 2008.

[158] "Ted O'Brien," Ballotpedia (online), accessed April 15, 2015.

[159] "New York's 25th Congressional District Elections, 2012" Ballotpedia (online), accessed April 12, 2015.

[160] "Facebook flashmob shuts down station, London, England," CNN.com, Feb 19 2009.

[161] "Ferguson Protestor's Medical Crisis at I-70 Shutdown Won't Damper Her Resolve," Danny Wicentowski, The Riverfront Times, Aug 11, 2015.

[162] "Here are the places Fergueson Protestors have shut down," Tasneem Raja, MotherJones.com, Dec 3, 2014.

[163] Andrew Cuomo's Pot Problem, Nick Pinto, Rolling Stone (online), June 9, 2015.

[164] Larson, Edward J.; Winship, Michael P. (2005). The Constitutional Convention: A Narrative History from the Notes of James Madison. New York: The Modern Library. ISBN 0-8129-7517-0.

[165] "The Constitutional Amendment Process", United States National Archives (online), accessed Nov 17, 2015.

[166] "Debates in the Federal Convention of 1787: Monday, May 28", James Madison, Teaching American History (online), accessed Nov 19, 2015.

www.ingramcontent.com/pod-product-compliance
Lightning Source LLC
Chambersburg PA
CBHW050117280326
41933CB00010B/1140